CHANGING
GEOGRAPHY

SERIES EDITOR: **JOHN BALE**

Regenerating city centres

**JANET SPEAKE
AND
VIVIEN FOX**

Geographical
Association

ACKNOWLEDGEMENTS

The authors would like to thank Dr Duncan Light for providing detailed comments on the Bucharest case study.

AUTHORS: Janet Speake is Associate Dean of Arts and Sciences and Vivien Fox is Director of the Centre for Health, Environment and Well Being at Liverpool Hope. They co-ordinate and teach on Liverpool Hope's MA in Contemporary Urban Renaissance.

ISBN 1 903448 29 8
First published 2002
Impression number 10 9 8 7 6 5 4 3 2 1
Year 2005 2004 2003

Published by the Geographical Association, 160 Solly Street, Sheffield S1 4BF. The Geographical Association is a registered charity: no 313129.

The Publications Officer of the GA would be happy to hear from other potential authors who have ideas for geography books. You may contact the Officer via the GA at the address above.

Edited by Rose Pipes
Designed by Arkima Ltd, Leeds
Printed and bound at Stanley Press, Dewsbury

CONTENTS

EDITOR'S PREFACE 4

INTRODUCTION 5

CHAPTER

1. CHANGING CITY CENTRES 7

2. RESTRUCTURING CITY CENTRES 13

3. THE PIZZA EFFECT 21

4. WATERFRONTS AND FLAGSHIPS 25

5. RE-IMAGING CITIES 32

6. A CULTURAL REVOLUTION? 43

7. CONCLUSION 49

REFERENCES AND FURTHER READING 51

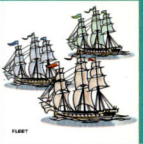

EDITOR'S PREFACE

The books in the *Changing Geography* series seek to alert students in schools and colleges to current developments in university geography. It also aims to close the gap between school and university geography. This is not a knee-jerk response – that school and college geography should be necessarily a watered-down version of higher education approaches – but as a deeper recognition that students in post-16 education should be exposed the ideas currently being taught and researched in universities. Many such ideas are of interest to young people and relevant to their lives (and school examinations).

The series introduces post-16 students to concepts and ideas that tend to be excluded from conventional school texts. Written in language which is readily accessible, illustrated with contemporary case studies, including numerous suggestions for discussion, projects and fieldwork, and lavishly illustrated, the books in this series push post-16 geography in the realm of modern geographical thinking.

The metamorphosis of the city centre is happening alongside changes within the contemporary city as a whole; changes which are associated with processes such as post-industrialism and post-modern urbanism. Such processes have transformed cities throughout the world and have encouraged geographers to rethink traditional explanations for, and means of analysis of, city form and structure. This book aims to help you explore the ways in which cities and their city centres are changing and to understand the nature of the fascinating ways in which they are developing. Because city centres are changing all the time there is always something in them that is new, exciting and different. There are also new ways to explain these constantly evolving patterns and processes.

John Bale
February 2002

INTRODUCTION

Many city centres in the more economically developed countries (MEDCs) are currently undergoing rapid, dramatic and distinctive change. The character of city centres in these countries is shifting from one traditionally associated with production and finance to one dominated by culture and consumption. In their function and form, city centres reflect both past and current trends in terms of their economic (e.g. retailing, telecommunications, leisure, culture), residential (e.g. high-quality private apartments, affordable housing) and social spheres (including work and leisure), as well as their general infrastructure (such as transport, utilities and premises). Such transitions have not generally been so marked in less economically developed countries (LEDCs) although cities such as Shanghai and Kuala Lumpur already demonstrate some of these processes and features of transition.

Whilst focusing predominantly on UK cities, this book includes references to other cities in Europe and in North America. It also presents case studies of the Central European cities of Berlin and Bucharest where changes have additionally been influenced by post-socialist transformations.

The changes taking place in city centres now are so notable and different from anything that has happened before that the process can be likened to a revolution, in this case one triggered and maintained by cultural change. Even the precise meaning of the term 'city centre' is becoming blurred. Traditionally it meant the very centre of the urban core which would have been surrounded by a zone known as the inner city. The urban core would have been distinct from the inner city by having the highest land values and the most prestigious functions and activities. Now, with increasing recentralisation and revitalisation, substantial areas of what was formerly considered the inner city are being regenerated in a way which includes many of these prestigious functions and activities. Differentiation between the outer city centre and the revitalised inner city is often difficult to discern. Hence, in this book the term 'city centre' is interpreted to include a range of central urban locations which function holistically as the contemporary city centre.

To aid your learning, Information Boxes are introduced throughout the text to highlight and add substance to specific issues, and Activity Boxes offer practical activities to help you to focus on and explore particular ideas.

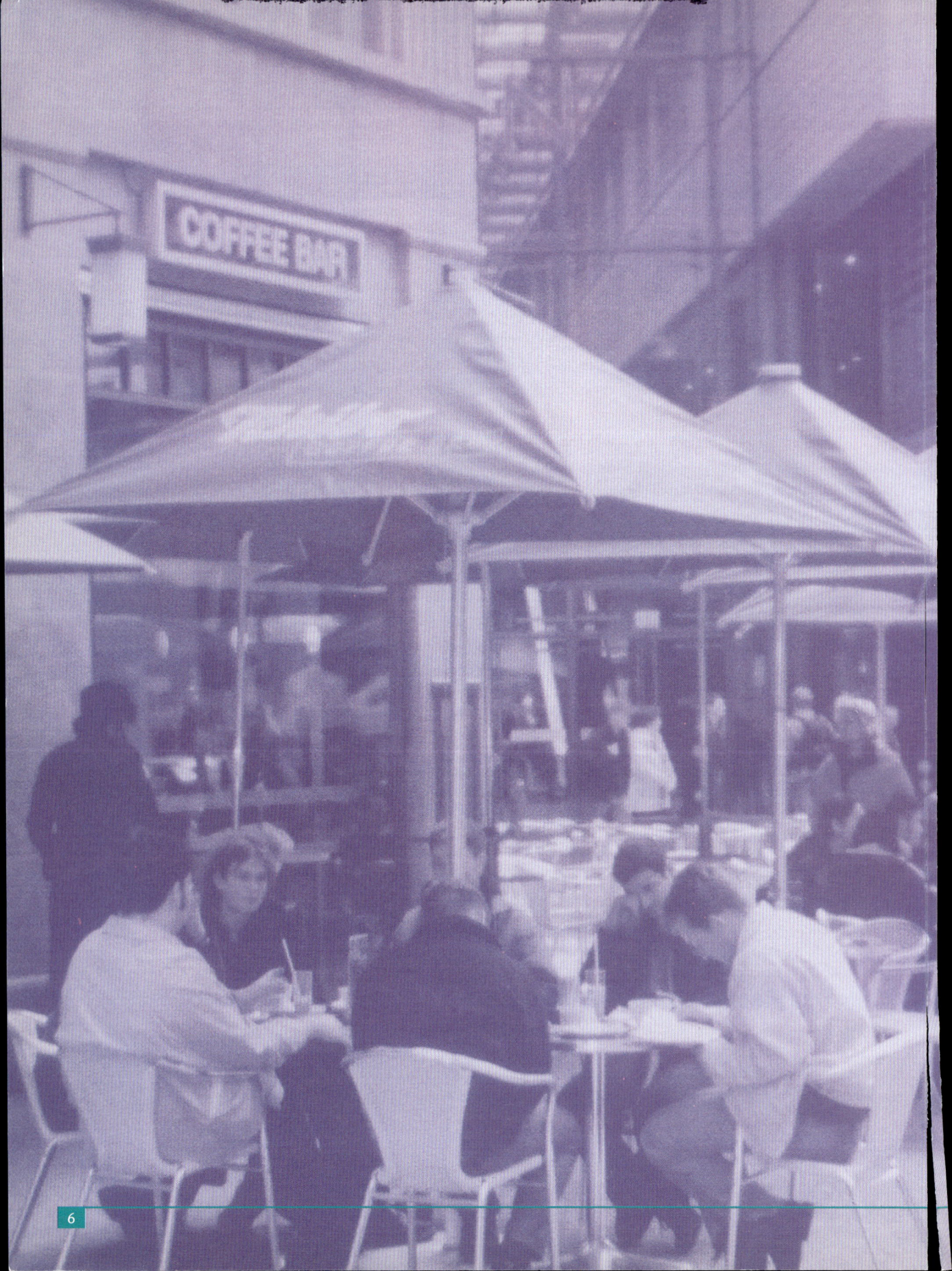

CHAPTER 1

CHANGING CITY CENTRES

The context

To understand fully the changes taking place in city centres, they must be seen in the context of change within cities generally. Such changes also need to be seen in the context of various, often interlinked, processes operating at different scales. These processes include the following:

1. *Globalisation* is both a concept and a process. The term may be used in this context to describe the way in which cities are shaped and influenced by factors operating at the global scale. One result of globalisation is that a degree of uniformity is apparent in many aspects of life in cities around the world – while they may differ in their detail, they have many characteristics in common (see points 2-6 below).

2. Since the 1980s the *information and communication revolution* has radically changed the way in which information is transmitted. The use of computers and the internet means that people no longer have to meet face-to-face in order to do business or share ideas and information. It also meansthat communication can take place simultaneously between places almost anywhere in the world. Such things as e-commerce, and tele-working, in which people work from home but are in contact with the wider world via the internet and video conferencing, both illustrate how it is now possible to operate effectively in a globalised society without necessarily living in towns and cities. However, cities and towns retain their importance as communication nodes, and may benefit in many ways from the growth of the communications industry. For example, the location of such industries in or close to cities brings prestige, employment and an increased demand for city-centre services and facilities.

3. *Competition* between cities to attract new investment is intense, both within countries (for example, in Scotland Glasgow may compete with Edinburgh), and between countries (Paris in France versus Amsterdam in Holland). To be attractive to investors, cities must be able to fulfil certain conditions, both economic (e.g. competitive land values, a skilled labour force), and social and cultural (e.g. suitable housing, leisure and entertainment facilities). Also, to be competitive cities need to have a distinctive and attractive image, and this is usually associated with cultural attributes such as architecture, art, cuisine and so on. Such cultural assets tend to be concentrated around the central areas of cities, or at least within easy reach of the centre.

4. *Footloose economic activities* are those which are not tied to a particular location by the need to be close to, for example, a source of raw material, labour or markets. Businesses which can be conducted 'on line' are examples of modern footloose activities, such as booking travel. The offices of such businesses can be located almost anywhere, so decisions about location may be determined by such things as the personal tastes and preferences of the employer or employees. For some trans-national corporations, a key requirement is to have a source of cheap skilled labour, so the location of their manufacturing units can be anywhere in the world where the necessary conditions can be met. This location may also change on a regular basis. In terms of their marketing and administrative elements, trans-national corporations require 'visible' and prestigious locations, and cities around the world compete vigorously with one another to be chosen. The so-called 'world cities' (Short, 1996), such as London, Paris, Tokyo and New York, are the most attractive and so the most successful in this regard, and play host to many major global businesses and decision makers. One consequence of globalisation is that the power of central and local governments is diminishing in terms of their influence on the decisions made by trans-national corporations about where to locate operations.

5. City centres are centres of *agglomeration*. Most businesses and economic activities display a tendency to cluster in order to obtain the

Activity Box 1: Linking city-centre activities with processes

Within any city centre, there are streets or areas that are devoted to certain activities or functions. These activities/functions can be related to the processes described above. Table 1 shows how activities and processes are linked in the case of Manchester city centre.

Choose a city that you know well, and produce a similar table for it.

For your chosen city centre consult the appropriate *Yellow Pages* directory and plot on a map the locations of ten examples of:

- Up-market designer shops
- Alternative lifestyle shops
- Theatres and concert halls
- Art galleries and museums
- Bars and clubs
- Recording studios/magazine or newspaper offices/television and radio studios

What patterns or clusters can you identify?

Table 1: Links between activities/functions and processes in Manchester city centre.

Activity/function	Location	Process
Up-market designer shopping	King Street North, Deansgate	Globalisation Competition Lifestyle
Multiple retail outlets/shopping malls	Market Street, Arndale Centre	Globalisation
Alternative-lifestyle shopping	Oldham Street	Lifestyle
High culture	Bridgewater Hall, Royal Exchange, Quay Street, Mosley Street	Competition Lifestyle
Popular culture	MEN Arena, Printworks, Great Northern, Deansgate	Competition Lifestyle
Gay Quarter	Canal Street, Chorlton Street	Lifestyle Agglomeration Competition
Chinatown	Portland Square	Lifestyle Agglomeration Competition
University sector	Oxford Road, John Dalton Street, Aytoun Street, Piccadilly	Agglomeration Competition
Legal and medical consultants	Great John Street, around Law Courts	Agglomeration
Information and communication technology	National Computing Centre, UMIST	Agglomeration Competition Globalisation Footloose
Media	Oxford Road, Quay Street, Castlefield	Globalisation Competition Agglomeration Lifestyle Footloose
General offices	Piccadilly, St Peter's Square, Babirolli Square	Competition Agglomeration Footloose
Loft living	Oldham Street, Bridgewater Street, Chepstow Street, Charles Street	Lifestyle Competition

economic benefits associated with agglomeration. These benefits include access to appropriate supplier and buyer links, and to support services such as accountants and lawyers, as well as to shops, banks and other facilities used by office staff. For some types of business, the city centre continues to be the most cost-effective location. Examples include financial and legal services, certain specialist retailers (e.g. designer clothes shops), and commercial enterprises such as advertising agencies. For such businesses, and also for certain cultural enterprises (e.g. clubs, banks, restaurants), ease of access for customers from a wide geographical area, and a large customer base, are seen as paramount.

6. During the 1980s and 1990s city centres became the focus for many changes that were taking place in *lifestyle expectations and consumption patterns*. Whereas the mid-twentieth century was characterised by decentralisation, as people and businesses tended to move away from city-centre locations, by the end of the century the trend had reversed. The re-population of city-centres has been due partly to the increasing availability of new housing on 'brownfield' sites, and also to the conversion of former industrial premises (e.g. warehouses, factories) into prestigious modern housing units. Closely associated with this residential development, and also with city tourism, has been the commercial rejuvenation of many city centres as the demand for services, amenities and cultural facilities has increased.

The city centre as a centre of consumption

One feature that most city centres now have in common is that they are dominated by consumption-driven activities, notably shopping, leisure and entertainment. People visit city centres to buy commodities of various kinds, some of which can be described as cultural commodities. Within this category are such things as film, art, music, food, literature and drama, all of which are provided in different settings and at different prices to suit a wide range of incomes and tastes. Figure 1 illustrates the leisure continuum from popular to high culture.

One aspect of the *commodification of culture* is the 'branding' of cities according to particular aspects of their cultural heritage. Thus, Liverpool city centre uses its 'local' music as a selling point to attract visitors, just as many cities package and sell aspects of their history through such things as heritage centres, exhibitions, historical tours and artefacts. Although this is not a new approach – city centres have traditionally provided shops and 'cultural' facilities such as concert halls, theatres, art galleries and museums, as well as restaurants, bars and dance halls – what has changed in recent years is both the range and balance of facilities and commodities on offer (see Figure 2), and more particularly, the rate at which these change.

Cultural commodities are subject to fashion and so change rapidly and often. For example, during the late 1990s there was a trend towards 'themed' bars (e.g. Irish), and towards restaurants and cafés selling particular types of food in 'ethnic' settings (e.g. Spanish tapas bars). What is 'in' one year, or even month, may be 'out' the next – the Irish pub that you passed last month may now have been converted to a vodka bar.

Changes to this cultural dimension of cities are often predictable – one example of this is the replication of successful ideas such as the seemingly endless number of café-bars – but this is not always the case. For example, an artist might set up a studio and, if his or her work becomes popular, other artists and art lovers will visit it. The studio may eventually turn into a popular attraction. Such developments are

Popular culture ⟶	High culture
Fast food	Haute cuisine
Chart-topping pop band	Shostakovitch
Musical	Performance of a Shakespearean play
Superlambanana – a contemporary sculpture in Liverpool (see front cover)	Leonardo da Vinci's 'classical' statue of David in Florence

Figure 1: Popular to high culture – the leisure continuum.

Nineteenth and twentieth century city centre	Early twenty-first century city centre
Economic activity based on the sale of manufactured goods	Economic activity based on the consumption of a wide variety of commodities
Retailing	Retailing
Cultural activities – celebrating the past (e.g. museums)	Cultural activities – celebrating the present (e.g. bars and clubs)
Finance and insurance associated with local and regional economic activity	Financial services associated with trans-national economic organisation

Figure 2: Contrasting functions of city centres – nineteenth to twenty-first century.

organic and apparently random. They can be witnessed on a small as well as a large scale (Case study 1 describes such change in one street in Berlin). You can investigate the change by using Activity Box 2.

This chapter has shown how city centres are changing to becoming increasingly consumption orientated. In the following chapters elements of changes and the processes contributing to them are examined in more detail.

Case study 1: Oranienburgerstrasse, Berlin

Oranienburgerstrasse is a street in the Mitte District of Berlin which was, until 1989, part of East Berlin. The street has experienced many changes, which mirror those that have occurred in the city as a whole, particularly in relation to its history of cultural diversity. For example, the street was a residential area for less affluent Berliners and for artists, and a centre for the Jewish community, up to 1942. During the Second World War the neighbourhood was extensively damaged and effectively left to rot. When the Berlin

Wall was demolished in 1989 and the city was reunited, artists, sculptors and those wanting to set up alternative clubs and bars gravitated to Oranienburgerstrasse, where at that time property was cheap. The street has a central location in the city and quickly became associated with a dynamic, individualistic culture. A derelict former department store became the base for several artists and sculptors working as a collective known as 'Tacheles e.V.'. It is interesting to note that 'tacheles' in Yiddish means

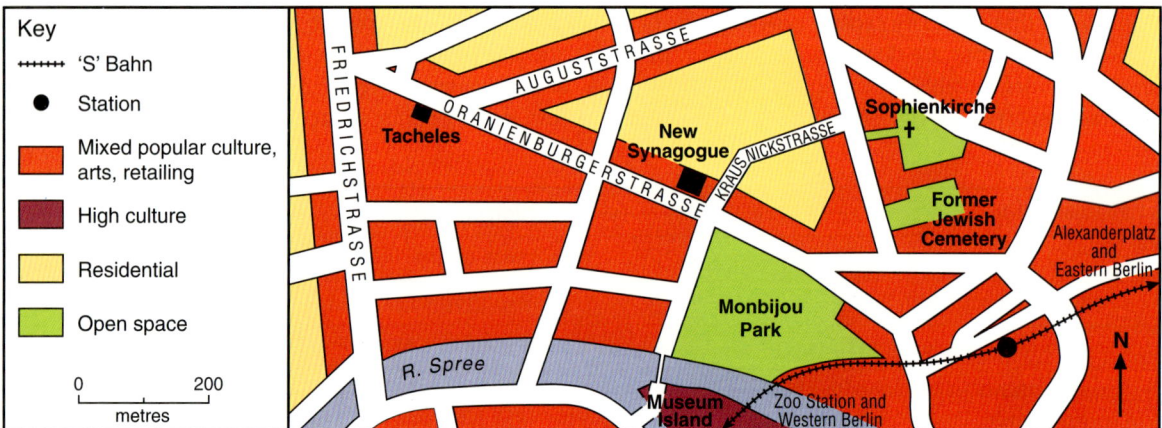

Figure 3: Culturally-led regeneration: Oranienburgerstrasse, Berlin.

Case study 1: Oranienburgerstrasse, Berlin (continued)

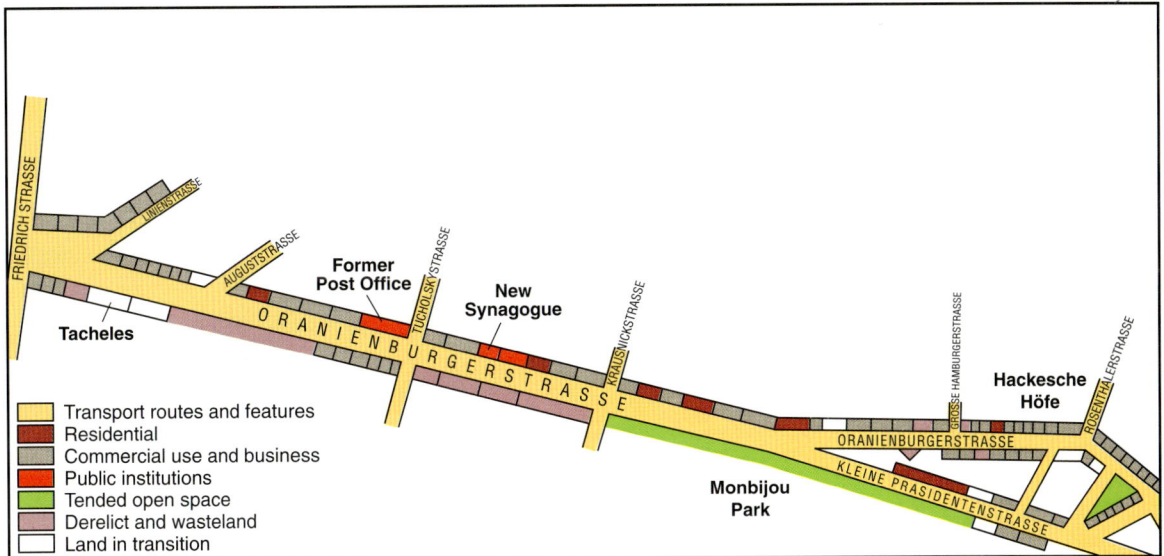

Figure 4: Major land use patterns in Oranienburgerstrasse, Berlin (derived from student field observations, 2001).

'let's get down to business'. This collective and its associated galleries and workshops is still known as Tacheles, and has rapidly acquired an international reputation. Thus, since the early 1990s Oranienburgerstrasse has become well-known for its alternative, 'bohemian' culture, including a 'graffiti café' (Figure 5).

Figure 5: The graffiti café at Tacheles, Berlin. Photo: Vivien Fox.

However, during this period the cultural development of Oranienburgerstrasse also began to diversify. Its popularity encouraged more conventional shops, bars and clubs to open up in the area. The renovation of what were once run-down courtyards (known as *hofs*, see Figure 6) also encouraged more up-market retailers to locate in the street, particularly on the north side, which now has a more conventional, conformist image than the south side, which remains more radical and 'alternative'. Overall, the street is becoming more mainstream, accepted and expensive (Figure 7), with the result that cultural innovators are choosing (and having) to locate elsewhere. Other districts of Berlin such as Prenzlauerberg are beginning to show signs of incubating new artistic talent and are taking on the role fulfilled by Oranienburgerstrasse a decade ago. In addition, Prenzlauerberg is already showing signs of gentrification and, such is the rapid pace of change, observers are beginning to ask themselves 'where next for the artists?'

Case study 1: Oranienburgerstrasse, Berlin *(continued)*

Figure 6: Courtyard or 'hof' at the rear of Oranienburgerstrasse (a) in 1992, and (b) in 2001, after renovation.
Photos: (a) John Davies, (b) Janet Speake.

Figure 7: Oranienburgerstrasse in 2001. Photo: Janet Speake.

Activity Box 2: Witnessing change

- Choose a city or a town that either you know well or that is well documented and locate an area within it that has changed during your lifetime.
- Use a range of resources – your own memory and that of elderly relatives or residents you know, written and/or visual accounts from the local studies library – to describe the main changes that have occurred in the area.
- Try to explain the changes in terms of what you have learned from this chapter.

CHAPTER 2

RESTRUCTURING CITY CENTRES

For geographers, change within urban environments generally is a subject of special interest and concern, and one which involves the use of a variety of models to help explain the dynamics involved. In recent years, given the kinds of changes described in Chapter 1, geographers have had to re-appraise the value of many existing models of urban form, and to look at new ways of analysing the contemporary city. Information Box 1 outlines the limitations of the models that are traditionally used.

What Information Box 1 makes clear is that traditional models of urban form do not offer a satisfactory means of demonstrating recent and current changes in city centres in the developed world. In particular, they do not accommodate the main processes which affected city centres during the last quarter of the twentieth century, that is the processes associated with the shift to the post-industrial city from the industrial city, and from modern to post-modern urbanism. In order to understand fully why the traditional models do not assist in our understanding of the contemporary city centre it is important to consider the nature of recent change in more detail. It is also helpful to consider these changes in terms of economy, society and culture and the physical make up of cities.

Economic restructuring

During the late 1970s and 1980s it became evident that western economies were experiencing the impacts of radical economic restructuring. Much of this change was attributable to the decline in the secondary sector (especially manufacturing industries). The locations which were hardest hit by this change were those largely dependent on manufacturing. Essentially these were the inner-city cores of large metropolitan cities in heavily industrialised regions. In the case of the UK, cities such as Manchester exemplify this trend. In Manchester, inner-city areas such as Beswick (once reliant on engineering industries) experienced major job losses. Between 1971 and 1981 there was a 58.8% decline in manufacturing jobs (City of Manchester Planning Department, 1986). At the same time as manufacturing industries were closing and/or contracting, the service industries in the tertiary and quaternary sectors were expanding. However, the growth of services largely occurred in locations which had not been industrialised, such as the suburbs of market towns in rural areas (e.g. Northampton, Yeovil, Shrewsbury). In metropolitan areas the growth in services could not offset the results of the massive decline in manufacturing, and the growth of service

---

Information Box 1: Traditional models of urban form

There are a number of limitations to traditional models of urban form, these include:

- Apply largely to the USA at a particular time (early/mid-twentieth century), e.g. Burgess, Hoyt, Harris-Ullman
- Assume a single, dominant central area, e.g. Burgess, Hoyt, Harris-Ullman, Mann
- Lack consideration of government intervention in urban change in, for example, planning regulations, transport policy, social housing, targeted investment, e.g. Burgess, Hoyt, Harris-Ullman, Mann
- Principal focus is residential land use, which is only one of many land uses, e.g. Burgess, Hoyt, Harris-Ullman, Mann
- Largely ignore physical setting of a city and its past land uses, e.g. Burgess, Hoyt, Harris-Ullman, Mann
- Do not allow for behavioural geographies of urban residents, for instance people's personal choices about where they want to live, e.g. Burgess, Hoyt, Harris-Ullman, Mann
- Cannot accommodate post-industrial city decline, e.g. Burgess, Hoyt, Harris-Ullman, Mann
- Cannot accommodate provision of land for socially desirable but unprofitable land uses, e.g. Burgess, Hoyt, Harris-Ullman, Mann

(Based on Kivell, 1993)

industries such as retailing tended to be concentrated in the urban periphery (e.g. Bristol, Newcastle-upon-Tyne, Sheffield).

For much of the latter part of the twentieth century, city centres competed directly with the outer areas of cities and were often the losers. Traditional intra-urban location patterns began to unravel as the effects of restructuring began to be felt. A distinctive characteristic of economic restructuring has been a change in employment patterns and practices. Regular hours of working – traditionally 9a.m.-5p.m. – were once the norm, but work patterns are now more flexible (e.g. variable shifts, flexible working hours), and part-time working is much more common – especially for women. These changing work patterns have enabled both manufacturing and service-sector industries to operate for longer hours for example on a 24-hour basis everyday of the week. In turn, this has meant that people need facilities, such as supermarkets, to remain open for when they are not at work.

Social and cultural restructuring

Up until the mid-twentieth century, the inner parts of many western cities contained a mixture of residential and industrial properties, with workers living close to their workplaces (usually manufacturing industries). Economic restructuring, particularly de-industrialisation of urban-core locations, resulted in the depopulation of city centres and inner city areas, in the growth of suburbs, and the development of the urban periphery. However, this trend has since reversed. As a result of both inner city regeneration and changing perceptions of what constitutes desirable living spaces and lifestyles, people are now moving back to live in the central areas of cities.

One aspect of the consumer society is that people identify themselves with particular 'aspirational' images or brands in clothing, household goods, cars, etc., and overall lifestyles. This often includes the places they live in. The recent surge in the number of residential properties especially 'lofts' and apartments in renovated former industrial buildings in city centres partly reflects this trend. People are attracted to live in what they perceive to be prestigious and fashionable places. In terms of living patterns, the trend away from the traditional nuclear family with two parents and children towards single-parent and single-person

households has had consequences in terms of housing preference. Converted inner city warehouses and factories are clearly being targeted at the single, the affluent and the young, thus resulting in radical changes to the demography of inner city areas. One consequence of these changes has been the exclusion of particular groups, such as those on low pay and the unemployed, from the increasingly affluent and gentrified inner and central areas of cities. It could be said that such groups are the victims of economic restructuring; they may feel marginalised, by-passed and excluded from contemporary city life. As a result, they may take to the streets in protest. This happened in Prenzlauerberg in the former East Berlin in the immediate aftermath of the removal of the Berlin Wall. Speculators had acquired property in the area in order to profit from its renovation, so local residents expressed their disapproval through graffiti and protests. Graffiti was a new form of expression for East Germans because such freedom of speech had previously been suppressed. The effects of the demonstrations were limited as gentrification has continued apace and the city authorities have cleaned up the graffiti.

Throughout the 1990s concerns were raised that there was increasing social segregation in cities and a widening of the gap (polarisation) between the social and economic 'haves' and 'have nots' (Wynne-Jones, 1997). It is often the case in western cities that affluent and less affluent neighbourhoods are located next to one other (juxtaposed) and the transition from one to the other can be very swift. Such juxtaposition can result in, or make worse, tensions between people – sometimes leading to protests and acts of violence.

Exclusion, threat and fear have all been associated with life in post-industrial cities, and fear relating to the perceived insecurity of public space is now reflected in the built environment. The use of 'fortress and bunker architecture' and construction of 'gated communities' for example Park La Brea central metropolitan Los Angeles is becoming more common. These and other approaches to reducing crime and the fear of crime are all designed to increase security for residents and businesses (see Information Box 2) (Speake and Donert, 1998).

Information Box 2: Characteristics of defensible space

Fortress and bunker architecture

Photo: Janet Speake.

Defensive architecture – high walls, few windows, extensive use of security measures such as impenetrable facades

Gated communities

Photo: Janet Speake.

Residential or other functions are enclosed and separated from the surrounding neighbourhood by walls and fences and other security measures. Access may be electronically controlled, e.g. keypads

Landscapes of surveillance

Photo: Vivien Fox.

The panoptic (all seeing) city. Closed circuit television surveillance, including mobile CCTV patrols

Carceral landscapes

Photo: Vivien Fox.

Prison-like urban environments. Minimal access points, usually controlled, highly visible security fencing or barriers, e.g. razor wire topped fencing or Loughrin palisade spike top fencing

Activity Box 3: Protecting spaces

Many building developments, whether residential, educational, retail, commercial, leisure-related or mixed-use, display elements of security and protection in their design. These features serve as much to enhance the legitimate user's sense of security as to keep out undesirable visitors (protective inclusion and explicit exclusion).

Using a base map of your school or college campus (or another small area of your choice) record security features that you observe, e.g. security fencing, CCTV camera, security guard, keypads or swipe card machines, controlled access.

On completion of the site survey, use your observations to complete the Protective Inclusion Explicit Exclusion (PIEE) Assessment. Two entries have been provided as exemplars.

Location	Feature	Protective Inclusion (PI)	Explicit Exclusion (EE)
Main entrance	Limited access entrance plus intercom to office	✓	✓
Edge of playing fields	Cobra-spike metal palisade fencing		✓

Compare your results with those of other students. You may find that you disagree as to whether a feature is protective inclusion or explicit exclusion or which is predominant. These differences of opinion could form the basis of more extensive group discussions on the issue of design and perception of crime or threat in contemporary urban environments.

During the last decade in North America and Europe, there has been recognition of the important role that communities play in determining the future of cities. As a result, emphasis has been given to community development, as exemplified by the Community Empowerment Zones in the USA. In Europe the trend towards development and regeneration through 'partnerships' of various interest groups has also meant an enhanced role for, and involvement of, community groups.

As an example, it could be argued that parts of Sheffield have been redeveloped at the expense of some of their residents. Broomhall is an inner suburb of the city that contains both large gentrified Victorian houses in private ownership and an estate of 1960s tower blocks and low level maisonettes. There was a problem of soliciting and kerb crawling in the area. The 'active', and arguably more affluent, members of the local community campaigned vociferously to remove soliciting (some of whom may have lived on the estate) and the police concentrated their efforts on removing kerb crawlers. The campaign succeeded and the prostitutes relocated to another area near the city centre. The Broomhall residents have been less successful however with their efforts to remove street parking by non-residents (e.g. students of Sheffield Hallam University (which is partly located in Broomhall) and staff at the nearby Royal Hallamshire Hospital) and to stop commuters using the local roads as a short cut.

Physical restructuring

During the last two decades, cities and city centres have experienced large-scale physical restructuring. This has been in response to a mixture of inter-related factors. Economic restructuring created tracts of derelict land formerly occupied by industrial premises and other industry-related land uses. The remnants of

■ **Activity Box 4: Looking at local a issue**

- Using local newspapers/news reports identify a particular issue affecting a local community. This may be a social, economic, health or environment related issue.
- Try and identify the area affected by the issue on a large-scale map.
- List the groups or organisations involved in determining the issue, e.g. Health Authority, local charity group, youth club, neighbourhood watch.
- On a second map identify the spatial area the group represents, e.g. a Residents' Association will have a clear focus based on named streets/roads.
- Compare the two maps you have produced. What patterns emerge? How much overlap or divergence is there? What does this show about community representation?

the old Victorian houses and the unpopular local authority housing stock from the 1960s and 1970s are often removed or refurbished. Cities were having to make themselves more competitive in order to attract inward investment.

In contemporary cities, decentralisation and recentralisation processes operate in tandem, resulting in the following clearly discernable trends:

- continued suburbanisation (though only for selected economic activities and the more affluent classes);
- a continuation of poverty and areas of disadvantage;
- selective city centre gentrification, in which certain areas have been regenerated – mainly due to wealthy individuals and developers purchasing and improving property for their own financial gain;
- general regeneration of city centre areas, involving a complex interaction between many agents of change including large corporations, local and central government and local communities.

Usually, the process of city centre regeneration takes some time to set in motion. However, in Manchester's case, the process was speeded up by the events of 1996, when an IRA bomb damaged part of the city centre. As a result of prompt action by government, developers and groups of local businesses and residents, large swathes of the city centre were rebuilt and business confidence restored.

The combined effects of economic, social and physical restructuring, as outlined above, can clearly be seen in western cities. Los Angeles is considered by many to be the archetypal (or classic) post-industrial/

postmodern city. Soja observes that 'what makes Los Angeles symptomatic of the new urbanisation is the magnitude and scope of urban change that has taken place since 1965' (1995, p. 128). He considers that Los Angeles has undergone six major restructurings:

1. Deindustrialisation of the economic base associated with changes in industrial production. The city's economic base is now centred on new high-tech industries, e.g. in Orange County and Long Beach, entertainment industries such as film making in Hollywood and low-tech craft based industries.
2. Globalisation – Los Angeles' development as a 'world city' and as a control and command centre for the Pacific Rim.
3. Decentralisation and restructuring of urban form associated with the redistribution of jobs and residents from central areas of the city to the suburbs and beyond, and the creation of an sprawling urban area which is a classic example of a 'galactic metropolis'.
4. Social fragmentation, segregation and polarisation generating a kaleidoscopic cityscape.
5. Breakdown of traditional political structures, rising levels of crime and the emergence of the 'carceral city' (Davis, 1990) in which combating crime through design and security features is generating a prison-like landscape (see pages 14-15).
6. Growth of urban hyper-reality in which 'fantasy worlds are experienced as if they were real' (Soja, 1995, p. 135). Not only is this reflected in Disneyland and Hollywood but also in themed shopping malls, bars and restaurants, office complexes and homes throughout the city.

The pace of change experienced in Los Angeles has been very rapid and the restructuring of the city, has generated new types of urban structure and characteristics. These changes are also visible in most other large metropolitan areas in the developed world, e.g. Tokyo, Amsterdam, Paris.

Returning to the question of urban models, the above points help to clarify why traditional models and explanations about how cities are organised, operate and change are no longer valid. It is clear that rather static models, such as those devised by Burgess, Hoyt, and Harris and Ullman (see Information Box 1), cannot take into account the dynamism of the processes involved. The explanations of urban change embodied in the ideas of modernism – which focused on the substantial role played by grand designs, centralised planning and breaking with the past (e.g. in terms of architecture) – were also considered too rigid and prescriptive. Post-modernism, which offers explanations (but no grand theory) and makes allowances for individuality even quirkiness and the unpredictability of change, has become accepted as a way of describing contemporary urban change (Information Box 3). This is because post-modernism can be used to describe the overall nature of urban change or the various components of urban life and fabric, such as architecture, art and music. You can investigate modernism and post-modernism by using Activity Box 5 in your area.

Patterns of urban form

Writing about post-modern urbanism in 1999, Ellin likened the effects to the impact of a tornado. Looked at on the ground, what is now evident in many city centres is a mosaic of land uses rather than large single-function zones such as those identified by early urban models. In today's cities, land use zones are smaller in scale and more fragmented. Changes in the patterns also occur apparently at random but with some regularity (rather like patterns in a kaleidoscope). Oddities and anomalies are commonplace – for example, in many UK cities it is not unusual to find a functioning nineteenth-century pub in the middle of a large expanse of derelict property on the edge of the city centre (Figure 9).

The early twentieth-century urban land use models spawned a new vocabulary to describe elements of the urban form, such as:

- *Zones* as used in 'industrial zones' or 'residential zones

- *Sectors* as in 'university sector' or 'business sector

- *Districts* as in 'shopping districts'

Information Box 3: The characteristics of modernism and post-modernism

Modernism, e.g. Milton Keynes 1970s	Post-modernism, e.g. Milton Keynes 2000s
Grand theory, e.g. New Town development according to Radburn principles of functional separation and distinct housing areas	Broad explanation, e.g. evolving more organically and less prescriptively
Centralised planning, e.g. largely public sector development	Individuality, e.g. more private sector involvement reflecting clients' specifications, more piecemeal development and more attention to the sustainability agenda
Uniformity, e.g. in building style within specific areas	Mixed (eclectic) styles, e.g. increasing architectural diversity within areas
Breaks with the past, e.g. modernist architecture and street planning throughout	Refers to the past, e.g. incorporation of vernacular styles in housing design
Stark and bold design	'Playful' design, e.g. shopping mall
Reality, functionalism, e.g. design of buildings reflected their use	Fantasy and imagination, hyper-reality, e.g. within the design of new buildings and public spaces

Activity Box 5: The characteristics of modernism and post-modernism

Figure 8: Characteristic housing estates: (a) 1970s modern style, and (b) 1990s post-modern style. Photos: Janet Speake.

Figure 8a shows a typical modern style housing estate dating from the 1970s. Figure 8b provides an example of a post-modern 1990s estate.

Choose two contrasting housing estates from the 1960s/1970s and the 1990s within your town/city. Complete the table.

Task	Estate 1 dating from 1960-70s	Estate 2 dating from mid-1990s
Describe the layout of the estate. Think about adjectives such as rectilinear, geometric, symmetrical, random, curving. Use other more appropriate adjectives if you wish.		
Were all the dwellings built at about the same time? Use archive maps and field survey to assess this.		
Describe the styles of the dwellings (including the building materials used).		
Do these styles show any references or links to the traditional architectural styles prevalent in the rest of the town, e.g. mock-Tudor?		
Rank on a scale of 1-10 how 'plain' or 'whimsical' the design of the dwellings is, where 1=plain and 10=playful.		
Rank on a scale of 1-10 how stark or imaginative the spaces between the dwellings are, where 1=stark and 10=imaginative.		

The two ranking tasks could provide useful indexes for comparing estates across or between towns.

Figure 9: An isolated pub at the edge of Liverpool city centre. Photo: Janet Speake.

Since then, new descriptive (often cultural) terms have been added to the vocabulary. For example:

- *Quarters* as in the 'Cultural Quarter', e.g. at Hanley in Stoke on Trent or the 'Jewellery Quarter', Birmingham. Interestingly, these often total more than four for any given city.

- *Villages* as in Greenwich Village, New York

It is evident that trying to construct a model to explain the complexities of these various characteristics of city-centre form is not straightforward. The model needs to be able to combine certain variables that are similar in all city centres with those that differ from city to city and which change over time. Chapter 3 illustrates one useful way of thinking about the form of the modern city centre by comparing it to a pizza.

THE PIZZA EFFECT

One of the most appropriate and fun ways of thinking about the form of a city centre is to liken it to a pizza. All good pizzas contain some ingredients which are common to all pizzas (e.g. the base), others that are found in most (e.g. tomato paste), and yet others that are particular to certain pizzas (e.g. pepperoni, ham). Translating this into city-centre terms, the base represents those parts that are common to all, for example the land and elements of the inherited built infrastructure (such as existing housing). The tomato paste represents elements found in most city centres, for example, green spaces, roads, hospitals. Toppings vary from pizza to pizza both in what they consist of and how they are arranged. These represent features particular to a specific town or city, for example, the Piece Hall in Halifax may be the olives or the New Town area of Edinburgh may be the pepperoni (Information Box 4). Use Activity Box 6 to develop your understanding of the elements of a town or city centre.

What the 'pizza effect' does is to provide a versatile representation of the fundamental characteristics of the city centre. This representation offers a vertical layering effect on a horizontal base.

Information Box 4: The pizza effect

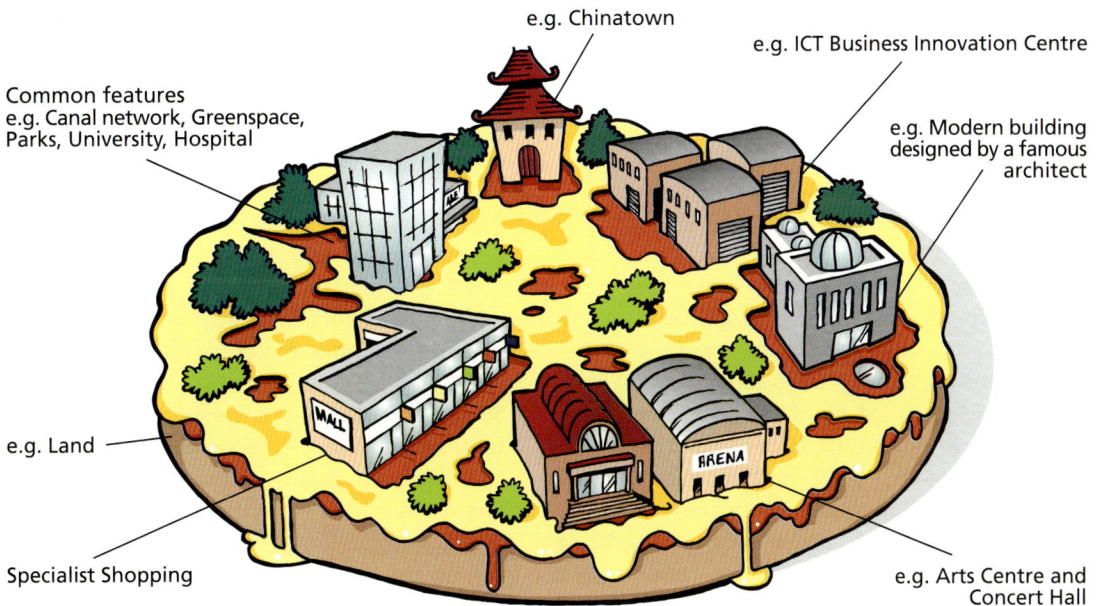

e.g. Chinatown

e.g. ICT Business Innovation Centre

Common features
e.g. Canal network, Greenspace, Parks, University, Hospital

e.g. Modern building designed by a famous architect

e.g. Land

Specialist Shopping

e.g. Arts Centre and Concert Hall

KEY

BASE	- Urban features common to all Cities/Towns.	
CHEESE/ TOMATO	- Urban features common to most Cities/Towns.	
TOPPINGS	- Urban features particular to a specific City/Town.	

Activity Box 6: Baking your own pizza city

- Obtain a large-scale plan of a city centre near your locality and draw a pizza-sized circle on it (it is entirely up to you whether it's an individual sized or family sized pizza).
- Using an A-Z of your chosen city centre, identify all the common elements (ingredients), i.e. the pizza base. If you prefer, shade these elements in one colour.
- Now locate the elements (tomato paste) that are found in most city centres (a *Yellow Pages* may be a useful resource here) in the same way.
- Finally, locate those buildings and features (toppings) that are particular your city centre pizza.
- Remember, you will need to devise a key and it may help to label the pizza toppings.
- Produce a display/presentation on the pizza you have 'baked'. You could include photographs or even scale models of specific buildings.

Now consider the following questions in relation to your individual pizzas and discuss them as a group.
1. Is there a clustering of any particular type of use or type of feature?
2. Are there any more patterns emerging, e.g. linear, regular?
3. Why do you think these particular activities might be distributed in this particular way?
4. Can you identify buildings that may represent the Central Cultural Heart?
5. Can you identify areas that are in transition – for example from obsolescence to renewed use, from one type of predominant activity to others, from open to gated communities?

Like pizzas, cities are multi-centred, multi-functional, multi-dimensional (in terms of markets and time) and in continuous transition; and their form results from both planned and random decisions.

What is very clear is that city centres, along with the other parts of cities, are flexible and adaptable. One of the characteristics of the contemporary city centre is the way in which the Central Business District (CBD) is being progressively transformed into the Central Cultural Heart (CCH). CCH is an appropriate term because, like a heart, it is the cultural activities that are currently giving cities their life blood. Traditionally the city centre was synonymous with high land values, leading to the agglomeration of businesses which could afford to locate there. This became known as the CBD. Now the land value structures of city centres are much more complex and fluid. Although many of the traditional uses may still be there, it is places and spaces which have particular 'currency' (i.e. they are fashionable and popular) that can command higher property or land prices. This popularity is frequently related to cultural activities and is therefore subject to the whims of fashion and trends (see pages 9-10). Thus, if fashions change, land prices could fall quite rapidly. In summary, much of the change from CBD to CCH reflects the transition associated with current cultural development and culturally-led urban regeneration.

City-centre regeneration

Many of the cultural activities present within city centres are new economic ventures which underpin the current revival of city centres, yet they may also represent the spearhead of culturally-led regeneration. In the urban competition between suburbs and city centres, until very recently city centres have been the losers. Subject to the twin forces of de-industrialisation and decentralisation city centres were unable to compete successfully, and both people and economic activities formed part of the general exodus from city-centres. To enable city centres to 'fight back', regeneration programmes have been devised and implemented, usually by city or borough councils. Such programmes are driven by policies directed towards employment creation through economic diversification, social inclusion and physical improvements.

Throughout the second half of the twentieth century the twin forces of decentralisation and recentralisation impacted upon city centres in a variety of ways. Information Box 5 shows clearly how the 1950s and 1960s the predominant movement was out of the city centre towards the suburbs and New Towns. Because much attention was being focused on out-of-town locations less emphasis was placed on the development of the central areas of cities. During this time many city centres displayed evidence

Information Box 5: Urban renewal trends 1950s-2000

Period	Trends in urban renewal	Impact on city centre
1950-59	Post-war rebuilding and mass house-building programmes	positive
	Urban sprawl and ribbon development	negative
	Introduction of green belts	positive
	New towns begin to appear	negative
1960-69	High density developments reflecting land values and new building technology	positive
	Total change in certain areas of towns and cities, e.g. city centre redevelopment, overspill estates, clearance areas	initially positive but later revealed to be negative
	Land use segregation	negative
	New towns programme continues	negative
1970-79	Obsolescence and dereliction in inner cities	negative
	Urban decline and social deprivation	negative
	Urban-rural shift	negative
	Small-area improvement schemes related to housing renewal	positive
1980-89	Major urban regeneration schemes, e.g. docklands developments, garden festivals, Urban Development Corporations	positive
	Partnerships between public and private sectors in urban renewal	positive
	Recentralisation	positive
	Impacts of globalisation and information and communications technology	positive and negative
1990-present	Continuation of concentrated deprivation (polarisation, segregation)	negative
	Continuation of under-used land resources	negative
	Property recession and homelessness	negative
	Public sector restrictions and increased role of private finance	positive and negative
	Continuing recentralisation	positive

of comparative decline. To combat this planning intervention moved towards targeted redevelopment of city centres through initiatives such as Urban Development Corporations, Neighbourhood Renewal Areas and Derelict Land Grants. Government (central and local) regeneration policies and programmes have largely concentrated on property-led and culturally-led regeneration – which are obviously not mutually exclusive. Property-led regeneration occurs when urban revitalisation is facilitated through the improvement of older properties and the construction of new properties (Figure 10). Examples of the former include the conversion of warehouses and industrial

Figure 10: Typical property-led regeneration at Albert Dock, Liverpool. Photo: Janet Speake.

Activity Box 7: Investigating reasons for change

Refer back to Information Box 5 and Activity Box 6. Repeat the pizza baking activity, but this time use the city centre as represented on maps, photographs, brochures and information from the 1960s or 1970s and the 1980s (you should find these sources of information in your local studies library).

Compare your pizzas and identify the trends they display. Consider for example:
- In what ways do the pizzas differ?
- Are there differences in the amount and shape of the base (thick or thin, soft or crusty)?
- Are there differences in the amount and spread of the tomato paste?
- Are there differences in the type and distribution of the toppings (basic Margherita or Pizza Deluxe with three types of olives)?

Using Information Box 6 and Figure 2 in Chapter 1 can you suggest which trends were operating and which impacts were experienced to account for the ingredients of your pizza and how they are arranged?

Figure 11: Typical culturally-led regeneration at Potsdamerplatz, Berlin. Photo: Janet Speake.

buildings into residential apartments. Culturally-led regeneration refers to urban revival which is brought about through, for example, sports events such as the Olympic Games, or the development of cultural amenities such as art galleries or places of entertainment (Figure 11).

Whilst in this chapter the focus has been on city centre form and general trends in urban renewal, Chapter 4 highlights the particular role of property led revitalisation often best exemplified through waterfront and/or flagship developments.

WATERFRONTS AND FLAGSHIPS

Waterfront developments

Deindustrialisation, recession, globalisation and the transition from production- to consumption-led economies have all contributed to the regeneration of cities. Some do so by making the most of what may have become obsolete landscapes. These include the waterfront areas that were formerly associated with industrial uses, such as former docklands, canal sides, lakesides and sea coasts (see Information Box 6).

The principal aim of waterfront revival is to regenerate obsolete (in terms of physical, function, image and location) industrial landscapes. This can involve the conservation of historic port environments (e.g. the Albert Dock, Liverpool), the creation of new functions and land uses (e.g. The Lowry at Salford Quays, Manchester), or a mixture of the two (e.g. Tiger Bay, Cardiff).

Use Activity Box 8 to investigate obsolete industrial landscapes.

The 1970s and 1980s were periods of active waterfront regeneration in many cities around the world. In the USA, the cities of Baltimore and Boston, both had extensive areas of disused docklands which were close to the city centre and provide interesting early examples of waterfront regeneration. Baltimore (Figure 12) began the process of regenerating its Inner Harbor in the mid-1970s, focusing on leisure facilities and the conservation of historic buildings.

Several large, up-market hotels were constructed to cater for visitors to the city (particularly conference delegates). Similar innovative waterfront revitalisation took place in Boston (Figure 14) during the same period. Here the focus was on leisure and retail facilities and the conservation and renovation of buildings – Fanouil Hall and Quincy Market, for example, have strong associations with the history of the city (especially in relation to the Boston Tea Party of 1773).

Figure 12: Waterfront regeneration in the Inner Harbor, Baltimore. Photo: Janet Speake.

Information Box 6: Types of obsolete landscape

Type of obsolescence	Features associated with it
Physical	Physical or structural deterioration of a building
Functional	A building or site is no longer suited to the function for which it was designed or is currently used
Image	The property or location is perceived as being less attractive and conveys an outdated, old-fashioned (rather negative) image
Locational	The location in which a building is constructed or business established is no longer appropriate for the activities that take place there

After: Tiesdell et al., 1996.

Figure 14: Waterfront revitalisation at Boston. Photo: Vivien Fox.

The waterfront developments in both these cities were judged to be highly successful and served as models for waterfront regeneration schemes elsewhere, including the Albert Dock in Liverpool (1981). The underlying aim of the early schemes was to make good use of large, often derelict, former maritime ports. As a precursor to even the Boston and Baltimore developments was the refurbishment of St Katharine's Dock in London. Although at a much smaller scale, the plans for the revitalisation of this derelict Dock infrastructure was commenced in 1969 but not fully realised until the mid-1970s. Both the St Katharine's and Albert Docks schemes involved the development of mixed residential and leisure uses in renovated former industrial buildings and docks.

Table 2: Obsolescence at East River, New York.

Type of obsolescence	Features associated with it at East River, New York
Physical	Disused factory, poor fabric, multi-storey building, poor communication between floors
Functional	Closure of manufacturing industry
Image	Outdated property
Location	Constrained site, difficult access, unattractive location

Activity Box 8: Investigating obsolete industrial landscapes

One example of an unimproved waterfront, as described in Information Box 7, is shown in Figure 13 and brief descriptions of the types of obsolescence apparent at East River, New York, are shown in Table 2.

Figure 13: The waterfront at East River, New York. Photo: Janet Speake.

1. Choose an undeveloped waterfront in a city centre and, if possible, visit it. If a visit is not possible, obtain photographs of your chosen waterfront.
2. Using Information Box 6, compose a table similar to Table 2 for the area/buildings/land use of your chosen waterfront.
3. Think about the opportunities the waterfront presents for regeneration and reuse. Be as creative as possible – an innovator not an imitator. Present your ideas in the form of a development brochure designed to obtain funding from business and government.

However, as Information Box 7 shows there are both positive and negative impacts of waterfront developments.

Later waterfront developments, such as those in central Leeds (Figure 15), Manchester and Birmingham, often focused on the revitalisation of inland waterways such as canals. What all these developments had in common was their focus on heritage, homogeneity and high culture. They typically included museums, galleries, leisure attractions, high-cost apartments, leisure-shopping and prestige office space. Battery Park City, New York, is another example of a recently developed waterfront where the emphasis is on prestige living. Information Box 8 lists the contrasts between the processes at work and their impacts in waterfront developments in the 1980s and the early 2000s.

At the beginning of the twenty-first century 'green' and environmentally aware projects, high and popular culture, 'imagineering' (creating fantasy landscapes) and the creation of spectacle are in vogue, whereas references to the past, heritage and post-modernist architecture are less fashionable. Contemporary waterfront regeneration now places more emphasis on cultural activities and the diversification of function, though residential

Information Box 7: Impacts of early waterfront developments

Positive	Negative
Conservation	Heritage tourism
Alternative uses	New city image
Flagship developments	Uniformity of 'heritage' image
Restricted type of use	Retrospective
Élitist	Top-down development

Figure 15: Development along the canalside in central Leeds. Photo: Janet Speake.

Information Box 8: Waterfront contrasts 1980s and early 2000s

	1980s	Early 2000s
Processes at work	Industrial decline Decentralisation Gentrification	Globalisation Cultural change Recentralisation Gentrification
Impacts of the processes	Residential Heritage Museums	Retailing Residential Hotels

Activity Box 9: Cape Town waterfront regeneration

Look at the map of the Victoria and Alfred Waterfront in Cape Town, South Africa on the website www.waterfront.co.za and use Information Box 8 to help you answer the following questions.

1. What are the predominant land uses within the Waterfront?
2. What is the evidence for the area's past economic activity?
3. What is the evidence to suggest that the Victoria and Alfred Waterfront is an early (1980s) example of waterfront regeneration?
4. What activities/functions do you think have been the most recent additions to the waterfront? Why do you think that they have been added?

Figure 16: Posters advertising the Mersey River Festival.
Photo: Janet Speake.

development continues to be an important element as does the focus on heritage in some cases. The current waterfront developments in Baltimore and Boston reflect these trends, particularly their orientation towards popular culture and leisure. Both cities have lively, vibrant, evolving waterfronts and use them as foci for festivals (e.g. the Baltimore Crab Festival). Other cities have used celebratory events to promote their regeneration activities (e.g. The Mersey River Festival in Merseyside (Figure 16)). Such innovative approaches provide a benchmark for successful waterfront revival elsewhere. In the UK, two highly successful recent developments have cultural activities as their focus, namely the Lowry Centre and the Imperial War Museum North at Salford Quays (canalside development), and the Tate Modern and Globe Theatre on London's south bank (riverside development).

The activities set out in Activity Box 10 are specially designed to enable you to investigate the functions of regenerated waterfronts of all types, i.e. riverside, canalside and dockside.

Regeneration is not a one-off process; for a waterfront area to remain competitive and economically successful, it will need to respond to changing fashions and demands. Thus, waterfront areas of the 'first generation' of revitalisation may need further development to maintain, or revive, their attractiveness. Light and Speake (2000) have reported a decline in the number of visitors to the Albert Dock in Liverpool and have identified characteristics that may no longer be quite as attractive to tourists (e.g. the shopping facilities) as they were when the Dock was first regenerated. In order to meet changing tastes, adjustments have been made to Albert Dock, such as the addition of new or conversion of existing buildings into hotels, bars and clubs. In this sense the Albert Dock like many other earlier examples of regeneration is undergoing a process of 're-regeneration'.

One thing that most regenerated waterfront areas have in common is that they involve a significant element of residential development of various kinds. Property developers exploited these areas, either by building new housing or by converting existing buildings (e.g. lofts in converted warehouses) or both. However, residential property is also vulnerable both to fashion and to physical deterioration and, in some of the first-generation waterside redevelopments, such property is already in need of renovation or refashioning.

Flagship developments

One of the key means of encouraging the economic revival of city centres is through the development of so-called 'flagship' projects. These are usually large-scale, high-investment projects such as major new museums, art galleries, theatres and sports facilities, which help improve the image of an area and attract people and other activities to it. Taking its meaning from the role of the flagship in a fleet during battle (Information Box 9), a flagship development is intended to lead and encourage other enterprises into an area with the intention of improving or changing the location's image and boosting its commercial success.

During the last 20 years there have been many flagship developments in the UK which have been introduced with varying degrees of success. Well known examples include:

- Scottish Exhibition and Conference Centre, Glasgow (Figure 17)
- Lowry Arts Centre, Salford Quays
- Millennium Dome, Greenwich, London
- Millennium Stadium, Cardiff
- Museum of Scotland, Edinburgh
- Tate Modern, Bankside, London
- The Waterfront, Belfast

Activity Box 10: Investigating waterfront developments

Note: Waterfront locations are potentially hazardous. Be sensible, take the necessary care and precautions when you conduct your fieldwork.

First decide on a set of land use categories. This will enable you to make a pilot (trial) survey of your chosen regenerated waterfront area (see Task 1). Choose your categories carefully, bearing in mind that most areas have certain features in common. You can, if necessary, revise your categories after your pilot study.

Now survey your waterfront using your chosen land use categories (see Task 2). You then record the results of your findings on a table (not a map), to show the main land uses found within your chosen area. Add a note on the evidence you used to support your decision.

Task 1
Think of the major different land/property uses that you would expect to find in your chosen waterfront area. These might include A: residential, B: retail, C: leisure, D: food and drink outlets, E: commercial, F: industrial, G: green space, H: vacant land.

These major categories can then be sub-divided to give a more realistic and detailed assessment. For example:

■ the residential category could be sub-divided thus: A1: apartments/lofts in converted old buildings, A2: apartments/lofts in all new purpose-built buildings, A3: terraced houses, A4: semi-detached houses, etc.
■ the retail category could be broken down into: B1: designer outlets, B2: convenience (food) stores, etc.

Compile a list that enables you to identify your major categories, sub-divisions and descriptions, for example:

Code	Label	Description
A Residential		
A1	apartments/lofts	in converted old buildings
A2	apartments/lofts	in new purpose-built buildings
A3	terraced housing	of a variety of ages
etc.		
B Retail		
B1	designer outlets	shops selling exclusive, designer goods, e.g. clothes
B2	convenience stores	shops selling food and goods for everyday use
etc.		

Task 2
Conduct a land use survey in your chosen waterfront regeneration area (this may include activities on the water itself, e.g. floating café-bar, houseboats). You do not need to record the use of every single building/site – the aim is to note the main functions in a given street or zone, and to construct a table (see below) which records your findings. Ensure that you record evidence to support your decisions about the choice of land use category. By observing properties and sites you begin to 'read' and 'interpret' the regenerated cityscape.

Location	Land use categories	Evidence
Dock Street	A1, A2	New purpose-built apartments (for sale notices), converted warehouses, curtains at windows, balconies with plants and wind chimes
	B1	Designer clothes shop (ground floor) with advert for art gallery on the first floor
Water Lane	H	Vacant plot with 'to let' sign
etc.		

Task 3
What are the main features of regeneration in your chosen study area? Summarise your impressions of waterfront renewal in your chosen study area

Information Box 9: Flagships

FLAGSHIP

large
expensive
state of the art
leads fleet
leads attack
bears the full force of attack
may be sunk
rarely retreats

FLEET

smaller ships
less costly to produce
less innovative
follows flagship
follows up with secondary attack
bears secondary force of attack
may be sunk
may retreat
one ship may take over the flagship's role

Sometimes flagship developments involve more than just one particular building – it may be the events associated with that building that act as the magnet. Major sports events such as the Olympic Games and the Commonwealth Games act as flagship developments for the cities in which they are located. They can also act as a catalyst for economic revitalisation, thus cities are intensely competitive in their quest to host major sports events. In the case of the Olympic Games the competition is at the global scale – Sydney, Australia, hosted them in 2000 and Beijing, China is to host the 2004 Olympics. Even where a bid fails, it may in fact raise the profile of a city and improve its chances of attracting other events. For example, although Manchester was

Figure 17: Scottish Exhibition and Conference Centre, Glasgow. Photo: Vivien Fox.

Activity Box 11: Flagship developments and their effects

Use the text in Information Box 10 to help you write a brief description of:

1. how a flagship development can help redevelop an area;
2. how a flagship development may attract other regeneration.

You should look on the internet for information about one of the flagship developments mentioned and relate your answers to 1 and 2 to it.

Make a list of other major flagship developments (anywhere in the world) that have recently been mentioned in newspapers, magazines or on the television. Conduct an internet search and/or consult other reference sources, to find out more about each one.

Using the example below, compile a table from the information you have gathered (add your own categories of information as required).

Name and location of flagship	Date of development	Name of architect/ development company	Cost of building	Source of funding	Distinctive characteristics, e.g. architecture/ function	Degree of success/ popularity

When you have found out information about your chosen flagship developments complete the following tasks:

1. Compare and contrast the cost of flagship developments.
2. What are the similarities/differences in sources of funding, e.g. government or private companies?
3. What are the similarities/differences in architectural styles or functions between your chosen examples?
4. Describe the ways in which your examples are similar or different in terms of their success/popularity.

unsuccessful in its bids to host the Olympic Games in 1996 and 2000, its international profile was raised by the process. One outcome of this raised profile has been that the city was successful in its bid to host the Commonwealth Games in 2002.

Flagships, waterfront revitalisation projects and other forms of culturally-led regeneration all contribute to changing the form and functions of city centres. The impacts of these developments can be dramatic and alter the appearance of a cityscape. As Chapter 5 shows, sometimes this new look can be used to create a new image for the city so that it becomes more attractive to potential business investment and visitors.

RE-IMAGING CITIES

During the last two decades, culturally-led regeneration has been used to spearhead the process of city centre revitalisation. This has involved the construction of new 'arts' buildings (galleries, museums, concert halls, theatres, etc.), or the conversion or major renovation of existing buildings. Some of this has been on a scale similar to that undertaken during the Victorian period when many of the existing arts buildings in western cities were first built. Examples of new 'arts' buildings include the Guggenheim Museum of Modern Art in Bilbao, the Jewish Museum in Berlin (Figure 18a), the Lowry Arts Centre in Salford, and the Royal Armouries in Leeds (Figure 18b). A major objective of these new centres is to 're-image' the cities in which they are built, raising their national and even international profiles, and assisting in their economic regeneration by attracting tourists and inward investment of various kinds.

Innovative architecture

One of the keys to the success of projects such as those mentioned above is the architecture of the new buildings. So important is the design factor to the success of new public buildings that local and national governments often stage architectural competitions, hoping that this will encourage architects to produce innovative and exciting designs. Such competitions have been launched for a wide range of buildings and structures including bridges, stations, parliament buildings and even bus shelters, as well as art galleries and museums. The Tate Modern, one of London's most successful recent cultural projects, is the result of such a competition. Architects were invited to produce ideas for the conversion of Bankside power station into an art gallery. The winning architectural practice was the Swiss based Jacques Herzog and Pierre de Meuron. The success of the project, which was part of a regeneration scheme for the south bank of the Thames, is arguably as much to do with the spectacular nature of the converted building as it is to do with the art works that it contains.

The same is probably true of the Guggenheim Museum of Modern Art in Bilbao, a completely new purpose-built gallery designed by Frank Gehry, and also of Gehry's earlier Frederick P. Weisman Art

Figure 18: New 'arts' buildings: (a) The Jewish Museum, Berlin, and (b) The Royal Armouries Museum, Leeds.
Photos: (a) Vivien Fox, (b) Janet Speake.

Museum in Minneapolis. Other architects have made use of the steel plating which characterises Gehry's buildings, for example Wilford's new Lowry Centre in Salford and McDougall and von Hartel Trethowan's National Museum in Canberra, Australia. In 2001 Liverpool also investigated the possibility of developing its own steel-clad 'Guggenheim' close to the Liver Building on the waterfront. Such developments have encouraged some people to ask whether a city is quite complete unless it has its own steel-plated, irregularly shaped building!

There are always risks attached to regeneration projects that depend on arts centres (new or renovated) as the focus of attraction, and some fail. Examples of recent problems in the UK are the National Centre for Popular Music in Sheffield, which closed after just six months. It subsequently reopened under new management, but is still experiencing operational difficulties. In the case of both the Royal Armouries Museum in Leeds and the Millennium Dome in London, visitor numbers were much lower than originally envisaged. There are many reasons why such ventures fail, not least because there are too many of them which results in a kind of 'modern arts centre fatigue'.

Striking architecture, which becomes closely associated with a particular place, is known as 'signature' architecture. Almost every city in the world has at least one building or structure that is very closely associated with its overall image. It is possible that cities can have multiple signature buildings from different periods. For example, Paris has the Eiffel Tower built in 1889 for the Exposition Universelle and the Pyramid which was added as an entrance to the Louvre Museum in 1989 (Figure 19).

Even smaller urban centres in the UK are acquiring a nationally recognised or signature building as part of their regeneration schemes. For example, Halifax's Dean Clough Centre, a converted former textile mill, is now home to an art gallery, cafés, shops and workshops, and the Tate St Ives in Cornwall is intended to blend with the seafront architecture, but is a distinctive building in itself.

Signature buildings and modern arts centres can be very significant in the process of culturally driven regeneration and the imaging of cities. However, there are other ways in which a city can attract attention to itself and enhance its image – public art, café bars and the concept of 24-hour cities are all examples of imaging.

Figure 19: Signature buildings in Paris from different periods: (a) the Eiffel Tower, built 1889, and (b) the Pyramid, built 1989. Photos: Diane Wright.

Public art

The introduction of various forms of contemporary art into streets, parks and other public spaces (i.e. public art) has transformed the appearance of many city centres and has raised their national and international profiles. Public art is not in itself a new idea: Rome and Helsinki have long been known for particular works of public art (e.g. the Trevi Fountain in Rome, the commemorative sculpture for the Finnish composer, Sibelius, in Helsinki (Figure 20)). However, each generation brings new ideas on how to promote or enhance the image of a place through works of art. One of the best known features of Chicago is a sculpture by Alexander Calder, and in Birmingham both Antony Gormley's 'Iron Man' and Raymond Mason's 'Forward' are strongly associated with the regenerated city. Sculptures and other forms of public art, such as murals, are usually introduced to provide talking points, create meeting places and generally add a 'different' dimension to urban space. At the end of the 1990s the introduction of a sculpture in Liverpool called 'Superlambanana' (see front cover and page 2) generated much discussion and controversy as it was (intentionally) moved from one city-centre location to another.

Much public art is commissioned by agencies involved in city centre regeneration, but there are also examples of less formal and non-commissioned art. Graffiti, for example, features prominently in some cityscapes and has become closely associated with those cities' images. Some graffiti 'art' is both complex and symbolic, for example, the graffiti on the remnants of the Berlin Wall in Germany has special significance. Figure 21 shows some of the graffiti on the East side of the Berlin wall, which until 1989 was completely inaccessible therefore untouchable.

Figure 20: Helsinki's commemorative sculpture to Sibelius. Photo: Vivien Fox.

Figure 21: Graffiti on the east side of what remains of the Berlin Wall. From left to right: general vandalism, mural art form, and far right – a political statement which translates as 'Many small people in many small places do many small things which can alter the face of the world'. Photo: Janet Speake.

Activity Box 14: The geography of graffiti

As Figure 21 indicates it is possible to consider 'graffiti' as generally falling into one of four categories:

1. Political statement, e.g. slogans.
2. Territorial signifier, e.g. in areas where gangs might identify their 'turf' or graffiti artists their signature or symbol.
3. Urban art, e.g. murals.
4. Vandalism, e.g. 'Kirsty 4 Jason', or 'Jaz woz ere'.

On a separate sheet of paper, draw your own illustration of what each type of graffiti might look like. In groups or individually, think about where you have seen these types of graffiti, on a motorway bridge in the city centre, on a gable end of a house in the inner city, etc. Try to identify both the surface used for the 'artistry' and the location within the city. The latter could be by name of district or estate or by a locational-descriptor as in the Berlin Wall example.

Consider which urban issue(s) this geography of graffiti reflects or relates to, for example, does it represent proposed property development, racial tensions, social exclusion, community art schemes or is it vandalism?

The rise of café-bar culture

A significant feature of recent city centre development has been the rapid expansion in the number of cafés and bars. While the café-bar culture is long-established in many European cities, it is relatively new to (and has been especially rapid in) the UK. Typically, in the UK, modern cafés and bars tend to be found in premises that were formerly occupied by 'high street' shops, banks or buildings societies. This rise in the so-called 'cappuccino culture' (Zukin, 1996) has played a significant part in revitalising parts of cities that were previously in decline. Cafés and bars can therefore act as catalysts for other commercial developments, in much the same way as flagship buildings (see pages 28-31).

Activity Box 15: Investigating café-bar culture

Think about an area of a city centre you have known well for some years in relation to the following:

■ In the last few years, have any new cafés or café-bars opened there?
■ If so, list them and for each one say what the building was used for before.
■ Describe the ways in which these new cafés and bars have changed the area.
■ In your opinion is the area better or worse than before? Give reasons for your answer.

A number of cities in the UK now have highly developed café-bar cultures. One of the most successful is in Leeds. An area of former warehousing next to the River Aire, known as 'The Calls', has been revitalised through the development of bars, clubs, restaurants and exclusive hotels.

The rise in popularity of cafés and bars draws people both during the day and in the evenings. Thus, it helps attract visitors to the city centre 'around the clock' and has become a distinctive feature of contemporary culturally-led urban regeneration.

The 24-hour city

Examples of fully developed '24-hour cities', in which most types of service are available round the clock, are still not common, though New York and Berlin come close to meeting this definition. Nevertheless, in most cities it is increasingly possible to find entertainment and to be able to shop, eat and drink (Figure 22) at any hour of the day or night.

In the UK, cities such as Glasgow, Nottingham and Cardiff aspire to becoming 24-hour cities, the main motive being to strengthen the local economy and generate new jobs. In Britain, it is estimated that the 'nightclub industry' alone is worth £2 billion a year (Malbon, 1998), and where there are nightclubs and late-opening bars and restaurants there will also be a demand for related services such as late-night transport (taxis, buses, trains), convenient car parks and access to banking services and shops.

Figure 22: Open all hours: shopping mall in Berlin. Photo: Janet Speake.

A common perception of the city centre at night is that it is a deserted, lonely, threatening and unsafe place to be. However, as more amenities stay open at night, and as 24-hour services become more common, such perceptions are changing (Oc and Tiesdell, 1997). Indeed, the main attraction of some city centres or central areas is the night life. Such cities are often referred to as being 'grimy by day and glamorous by night' – Leicester Square in London is one example.

Activity Box 16: 24-hour cities

As the table below indicates, some services are better suited to 'round the clock' provision than others.

Better suited	Less well suited
Clubs	Professional services, e.g. accountants
Libraries	Shops
Medical provision	
Security services	

- Explain why you think some services are better suited to 24-hour provision than others.
- What other activities might you include under each heading? Complete the table and add extra rows if necessary.
- How do you think that the increase in the number of activities operating 24 hours a day might affect the people who live in the area?

Activity Box 17: Security cameras

Think of a journey you might make from home to your nearest town/city centre. List the various spaces you would use where you may be monitored on a security camera or where security cameras may be visible.

Now make the journey and note where CCTV cameras are actually in evidence.

- How close was your estimate to reality?
- How do you feel about being watched in this way?

An important element in the process of city centre regeneration is the introduction of security measures, such as closed circuit television (CCTV) which has been found to help prevent crime. Where public spaces like roads and streets are under surveillance it is less likely that they will become the territory (or 'turf') of gangs. This stops them becoming the 'privatised' space of such gangs who 'defend' their space against people venturing into it. The use of security systems in city spaces and buildings works in two ways, it makes them safer places to *be* and it makes people *feel* safer. This, coupled with an increase in 24-hour facilities, has helped to rehabilitate city spaces that were once considered 'no go' areas.

There are some cities, notably Las Vegas in the USA, where casinos and other entertainment facilities operate on a 24-hour basis. In Britain, there are some towns and cities where round the clock attractions of this kind are being actively encouraged as part of a regeneration strategy. One example is Blackpool, a seaside town which has long been known for its evening as well as daytime entertainment facilities, but which is seeking to reinvent itself (see Case Study 2).

Residential revitalisation

A very significant goal of inner city regeneration programmes has been to attract people to live in central areas, as well as to go there for work and entertainment. Since the 1970s and 1980s, this has been achieved to a great degree, as exemplified by Manchester where the number of city centre residents rose from about 1000 in 1991 to an estimated 10,000 in 2000.

This revival in city-centre living is due to many inter-related factors. Crucial among these have been the construction of new housing, and the conversion of former commercial and industrial buildings into residences, both designed to appeal to the younger, more affluent end of the market. Characteristic of the first phase in such developments was the conversion of obsolete old buildings into trendy apartments known as 'lofts'. Residents were supplied with basic services such as water and electricity but could design the interior spaces according to their own tastes. Later developments have tended to involve full-scale conversions by property developers, though the resulting residences may still be referred to as 'lofts'. Certainly, loft living has a fashionable image (Zukin, 1996) and has encouraged revitalisation of older buildings even in otherwise run-down areas.

Another stimulus for inner city residential development has been the rise in the demand for purpose-built student accommodation particularly for universities and colleges located in the city centres (e.g. Nottingham, Liverpool, Manchester). This has often been achieved through the conversion of older buildings into small living units, or the renovation of high-rise blocks or new build.

Where new housing has been built in central areas, it has been designed to cater for specific markets, and in particular for young, single people. Young single people are most likely to take advantage of the cultural opportunities developing in city centres, and by moving into these areas will encourage the process of regeneration as they demand local services and amenities. These inner city residents may also work within the city centre, thus their journey to work is likely to be short and involve walking or the use of public transport. Indeed, some local authorities have devised housing strategies to reduce traffic congestion in city centres. In Edinburgh and in the Borough of Southwark (London), the authorities have built inner-city housing estates where a condition of residence is non-ownership of a car.

Another process that has accelerated the regeneration of inner city areas is gentrification. Most often this involves transforming former working-class houses into ones that are attractive to the modern city dweller. As these 'gentrified' houses

Case study 2: Blackpool case study

Figure 23: Blackpool Leisure Beach. Photo: Janet Speake.

Blackpool has been a popular tourist town since the eighteenth century and it is now one of Britain's most famous seaside resorts, catering for more than 12 million visitors a year. With 91,000 bed spaces, and a wide range of traditional seaside holiday entertainment on offer, Blackpool is reckoned to generate about £545 million a year from tourism. However, like many other British resorts, it has experienced a downturn in visitor numbers since the 1990s. This is due, in part, to its failure to readjust to the changing tastes and demands of its potential visitors.

For example, Blackpool has for years been geared to catering for people who make repeat visits, and traditionally these have been families. As a result the town lacks the necessary infrastructure to cater for young people and the singles market, e.g. for stag nights and hen parties. It also does not have the infrastructure for the developing market in short breaks, which requires a higher quality of accommodation and facilities than those currently on offer, for example, only 8000 of the resort's bed spaces are of three- or four-star quality.

Compared with other towns in Lancashire, Blackpool's population has fewer people in the 'economically active' category and more in the 'transient' category (i.e. visitors). Its economy is comparatively undiversified in that 87% of jobs (46,400) are in the service sector (which includes tourism and leisure).

Blackpool is the twelfth poorest area in the UK in terms of gross domestic product per person (£7383), which is 69% of the UK average. Unemployment rates are usually higher than the regional and national averages, and the income level of nine out of ten residents in central Blackpool is below the low pay threshold. The 1998 Index of Local Deprivation showed that Blackpool ranked 51 out of 326 Local Authority Districts in the UK (Blackpool City Council, 1999).

In 1996 the town (through the Blackpool Challenge Partnership (BCP)) was successful in its bid for Single Regeneration Budget 2 funding which has been used to support urban regeneration in relation to four areas: economy, training, housing and community. Part of this funding has been used to develop Blackpool Business Park and Blackpool Technology Park in an attempt to diversify the town's economy. Since then the BCP has bid for SRB Round 6 funding and has made a case for European Union Objective 2 funding.

The BCP's vision for the future of the town is one in which 'Blackpool will be recognised as a vibrant, inclusive and prosperous town where visitors and residents share the common goal of Blackpool being the number one visitor destination in the UK'.

However, the regeneration initiative that received greatest national publicity during 2000-01 was the proposal by Leisure Parcs to open six casinos in Blackpool. Leisure Parcs submitted its plan to the Gambling Review Body (GRB). The aim behind the proposal was to revitalise the town as a major gambling centre, as suggested by headlines such as 'Welcome to Vegas-on-Sea' (Holden, 2001) and 'Blackpool gambles on becoming a Lancashire Las Vegas' (Fawcett, 2001). In July 2001, the GRB recommended the easing of existing UK gambling laws to facilitate such developments.

While the comparison with Las Vegas may be apt, it is to another US city that Blackpool might turn for a more appropriate role model, namely Atlantic City, New Jersey. This city developed last century as a popular seaside resort, and, for the same reasons as Blackpool, has diminished in popularity. In 1977 the State of New Jersey introduced the Casino Control Act to authorise casino gambling in Atlantic City. Gradually, the number of casinos increased and now Atlantic City has 12 casinos, 145 gaming tables and 32,500 slot machines which produce an income of US$4 billion, contribute US$450 million in tax, attract 34 million visitors a year and employ 50,000 people (Taylor, 2000). In Blackpool, the Leisure Parcs plan is targeted towards fuelling regeneration through gambling, but not at the expense of traditional visitors. It is envisaged that the first of the six planned casinos, Pharaoh's Palace (a 'themed', 1000-bed centre on a 10-acre site), will be in operation by 2004. Marketing of the casinos will be both UK and internationally oriented, with Manchester International Airport serving as the European gateway.

Activity Box 18: Urban re-imaging

During the 1990s there have been changes in the types of urban activities portrayed in publicity materials, e.g. shifts from heritage-centred images to more culturally-focused images. Sources such as websites, visitor guides and information packs indicate how cities 'sell' themselves to tourists, visitors and prospective investors. Information produced by various organisations for the attraction of tourists or businesses often reflects current urban trends. Publicity materials may be used to

- identify what cultural images are conveyed
- determine if the cultural images are the predominant images, for example how do they compare to the number of images promoting the town's history?
- compare urban images through time i.e by consulting past publicity materials

Choose one form of publicity material for Blackpool, e.g. websites (see www.blackpooltourism.com and www.blackpool.gov.uk) or tourist information brochures and assess the images it projects of the town.

Image of town	Assessment of images
General overview Does the town present itself as a seaside resort or an urban centre?	
Tourist overview Is the focus on the historic nature of the town, on its culture and/or sports? Which markets (e.g. young single people, families) are targeted?	
Description of buildings Is the emphasis on historic or new buildings?	
Types of visitor attractions	
Types of sports facilities	
Types of cafés/restaurants	
Types of theatres/cinemas/clubs	
Images of retailing portrayed (e.g. specialist shops, up-market boutiques)	
Hotels What types of hotels are shown?	
Major businesses Are these commercial and/or industrial?	
Transport infrastructure	
Distinctive areas (e.g. promenade)	
Other characteristics (e.g. proximity to countryside)	

Consider your assessment of the images in relation to Case Study 2.
Now complete the sentence, 'Blackpool is ...'

become more fashionable they rise in price, and can only be bought by people with a high disposable income. As the population becomes more affluent, so the demands it makes on the local area in terms of services and amenities will change and thus affect the whole infrastructure. (Islington in London is one example of a 'gentrified' area). For example, an area that once contained convenience shops and other amenities serving the local community, may, after gentrification, lose these amenities as designer shops, more expensive restaurants, delicatessens and other up-market outlets take their place (see Information Box 10).

Inevitably, there are winners and losers as a result of gentrification, and often some of the changes involved are strongly resisted – particularly by those people who are forced to move out of the areas where they have always lived or worked. It may be necessary for such people to do so because of increases in local taxes or rents or because their homes are to be demolished. In the case of the Schönhauserallee area of Berlin (and other areas that experienced rapid redevelopment in the late 1990s in the city), local residents showed their disapproval of gentrification through graffiti messages such as 'speculators out' and 'yuppies out' (see also page 14).

One consequence of gentrification is that areas that were once mixed in terms of their social and commercial character become more uniform and more universal. This means that gentrified areas in cities as far apart as New York (e.g. Battery Park City) and Salford (e.g. Salford Quays) look very much alike.

This 'universality' of style has meant that cities around the world have had to try even harder to make themselves distinctive, and to 'market' those aspects of their character, such as cultural identity, that make them unique (see Activity Box 19).

Development of cultural identity

Ethnic diversity, both in terms of the resident population, and in the goods and services available, is a characteristic that most cities share. However, the mix and balance of different cultures tends to be different and distinctive in each case. It is now common in many cities to find 'quarters' or areas which are so strongly identified with a particular ethnic group that they have been given names such as 'Chinatown' or 'Little Italy'. Entering these areas is almost like entering a different country: the language, dress, goods on sale, and places of worship, etc., suddenly change, as if a barrier has been crossed. Such distinctive qualities give areas of cities a special character and quality, which can be used to attract tourists and inward investment.

In Liverpool, the Chinatown area around Duke Street in the city centre underwent a period of regeneration in the 1990s. The Chinese community was actively involved both in the process of regeneration, and with the strengthening of links between Liverpool and Shanghai, with which the city is twinned. The regeneration programme included a new Chinese cultural centre and the construction of a Chinese Arch at one of the main points of entry into the Chinatown area (Figure 24). As well as benefiting

---

Information Box 10: Characteristics of gentrified locations

- Converted formerly obsolete buildings, e.g. warehouses
- Renovated or rehabilitated older housing
- Newly constructed apartment blocks
- Up-market, specialised shops
- Expensive and/or fashionable restaurants and bars
- Residents mostly high earners

Activity Box 19: Investigating gentrification

- Where, in a town or city you know, has gentrification taken place on a large scale?
- What is the main evidence for it having happened?
- What are the main consequences for the area?
- In your view, have the changes due to gentrification been good or bad?

the local Chinese community, this has enhanced the city's image and encouraged tourists to visit the area. Such improvements are part of a wider scheme to revitalise the western fringes of Liverpool city centre by promoting certain 'quarters' in relation to particular cultural themes, such as Wolstenholme Square (the location of the club Cream) and Concert Square (where there are several bars and restaurants).

Changing city centre images

A hundred and fifty years ago a positive urban image for most of the UK's largest cities was one which emphasised industrial prowess and power. Cities such as Birmingham and Glasgow were proud of their reputations as world-class manufacturing centres. Birmingham was considered to be a city 'of a thousand trades', Manchester viewed itself as 'the workshop of the world', and so on. In those days, success was directly equated with industrialisation. During the twentieth century, as the relative importance of manufacturing within western urban economies dwindled, so too did its significance in the 'imaging' of cities. In fact former industrial cities sought to play down their image as manufacturing centres as industry became associated with negative images such as dirt, decline, dereliction, unemployment and poverty. Gradually, the images of success became associated with such things as high quality of life, ample leisure and entertainment facilities and a clean environment. One example is provided by Short (1996), who describes the ways in which the city of Syracuse in New York State changed its image from a city dominated by factories and industrial production to one celebrated for the high quality of its environmental setting.

By the end of the twentieth century, what most western cities are trying to do is promote themselves as exciting and different places to be, with the main focus now being on facilities relating to the consumer culture. For example, Edinburgh has developed an image of itself as a Festival city. Some cities have benefited from specific competitions such as European City of Culture, and UK City of Architecture and Design, both of which were won by Glasgow in 1990 and 1999 respectively. Glasgow also attempted to shake off its rather negative image and to become more competitive by adopting the slogan 'Glasgow's miles better'. It is important that self-promotion of this kind is linked to an image that the city can live up

Figure 24: The entrance to the Chinatown area in Liverpool. Photo: Janet Speake.

to in reality. This can sometimes influence how areas develop (Hall, 1998), i.e. if a city sells a particular image of itself (e.g. as an entertainment centre) then this itself may serve to enhance its ability to attract bars, clubs. The means by which cities can promote themselves include brochures, adverts, websites and so on, but cities may also be indirectly promoted when used as the context for a novel or travel book, a film or a television drama. Some cities now have a dedicated office that handles negotiations with film and television companies, including setting the financial terms for the use of the city as the setting for a film, a one-off drama or a series. Film is a very powerful medium, it reaches a wide audience, therefore, the portrayal of a city in a film can be influence peoples' image of it (see Activity Box 20). A positive, attractive image can boost the local economy in a variety of ways, not only through tourism but also by encouraging new businesses to locate there. Cities such as Dublin, Glasgow, Newcastle and Liverpool all have varied cityscapes which serve as dramatic backdrops for films. These and other former industrial towns in the British Isles are often used as settings for films with a strong 'social history' storyline (e.g. *Trainspotting* (filmed in Edinburgh) and *The Full Monty* (filmed in Sheffield)). In Liverpool, six movies were shot in 2000 alone, including *The 51st State*. The immediate

Activity Box 20: Representations of cities

Choose a city that you have *not* visited. Make a list of the books, films and/or television programmes you know are set there. For each one, decide if the image(s) of the city in the book, film and programmes are predominantly positive or negative.

■ How do these images match your own impressions of the city?

Now repeat the above activity for a city that you know well.

Choose one of your cities and decide how best to promote it to outsiders. You will need to consider the audience: do you want to write it for business people, potential residents or for tourists? Produce either a brochure, a website design, or the storyboard for a film to illustrate those aspects of the place that you think will be most attractive to potential 'customers'.

benefits of this were that actors, film crews and other related personnel boosted the local economy by staying in local hotels, eating in restaurants, buying goods in shops and so on.

The perception of place is very important. As this chapter has shown, your mental images of places are influenced by diverse media including contacts, experience and anecdotes. Chapter 6 intends to challenge some of your preconceptions about a post-socialist city in central Europe.

A CULTURAL REVOLUTION?

The term 'revolution' conjures up ideas of a radical change of circumstances, attitudes and conditions. For many cities the recent changes that have taken place within their centres have been truly revolutionary in economic and social terms, and in the ways in which culture in its many forms has become a leading force in the revitalisation of city centres. The legacy of the industrial era took time to shake off and up until the 1970s and 1980s the central areas of many cities were generally perceived as being in decline and unattractive compared with the suburbs, small towns and rural areas.

This idea of 'revolution' can be applied to city centres which experience rises in economic activity and prosperity as the economy turns in circles from recession to growth. It can also be linked to the way in which the cultural life of cities develops and changes in a cyclical way.

For some cities, particularly in former communist countries, e.g. Latvia, Estonia, recent changes have been associated with revolution in a real political sense and in terms of economic, social and cultural transformation. Case Study 3 details changes that have taken place in Bucharest, Romania. These can be investigated using Activity Boxes 20 and 21.

Case study 3: Revolution in Bucharest

With close to 2.5 million inhabitants, Bucharest is Romania's largest city. As the capital, Bucharest is also the political, commercial and industrial hub of the country. Like many cities in central Europe, Bucharest has experienced rapid and dramatic change. Much of this has taken place since the Revolution in 1989, when the country felt the impacts of the transition from a communist (centrally planned) to a capitalist (free market) economy (see Information Box 11).

Even before the Revolution, however, the built environment of the city was changing. In 1977 a major earthquake damaged many buildings, providing the country's communist dictator, Nicolae Ceaucescu, with the opportunity to remodel a large part of the centre of Bucharest as a showpiece communist capital city. In his visualisation of how the city should be reconstructed, Ceaucescu was much influenced by the modernist architecture and planning of North Korea. The changes were considerable, involving among other things the construction of the *Centru Civic* (Civic Centre) (presently unfinished) and the monumental Parliament Palace (the second largest building in the world after the Pentagon in Washington DC) (Figure 25), as well as the demolition of buildings in the Uranus and Vacaresti districts of the old city. This area, which occupied 5 sq km, included many of the city's

finest churches, monasteries and residences. As part of the redevelopment over 40,000 people were forcibly moved to the suburbs.

Following the Revolution, Romania reinvented itself as a democratic and capitalist country. This gradual shift was accompanied by privatisation and the emergence of some individual entrepreneurial activity (even things as simple as people making a living by refilling cigarette lighters, polishing shoes, washing car windscreens). But for the residents of the city of Bucharest, there was little obvious change. Transition came slowly, almost organically, as people began to experiment with setting up small businesses and shops, including kiosks on the city streets selling mixed goods ranging from lingerie to tobacco ('kiosk culture'). Thousands more individuals set up stalls selling a huge variety of mostly imported goods in an entirely unregulated way. There was little foreign investment in the city, although some of the city's hotels were privatised.

Due in part to increasing political liberalisation in the mid- to late-1990s, major changes began to take place in Bucharest. Several large trans-national corporations – notably McDonald's and Hilton Hotels – opened up in the city (the Hilton Corporation bought the Athénée Palace Hotel in 1995 for US$21 million (Burford and Richardson, 1998) and from then on the pace of change accelerated. As business people began to visit the city, so demand rose for various services and amenities, ranging from car-hire companies to banking and insurance. Air traffic flows increased at Otopeni International Airport necessitating the building of a new terminal building.

Information Box 11: Phases in urban development in Bucharest

Changes in...	Pre-1989: Communist regime	1989-92: The early transition period	1992-96: Capitalist transformation begins	Post-1996: Acceleration of capitalist transformation
retailing	Centralised planned, small retail outlets and some large but often empty state-run stores, some kiosks	Small retail units and a few trans-national corporations, e.g. Coca-Cola. The growth of 'kiosk culture'	Rapid development of 'kiosk culture' and trans-national companies, e.g. Benetton, McDonald's. Increasing growth of supermarkets. Emergence of an informal 'banking district' in the former Civic Centre	Mixture of retail outlets, decline of kiosks following their regulation. Introduction of shopping malls. Increasingly specialist and expensive shops to cater for both visitors and wealthier city-dwellers. Appearance of foreign firms
housing	Centralised, planned tower blocks. High-density housing. Little low-density suburban housing	Privatisation of state-owned housing (mainly apartment blocks)	Continuation of privatisation, growth of price differentials in the city. Demand for housing and office space by foreign companies	Increasing pressure on rural land on edge of the city. More building of individual houses in this area. Building of entirely new 'residential villages' for foreign businesses
transport	Centrally planned buses, trams, trolleybus, urban railways and the metro underground. Relatively few cars	Maintenance of public transport plus expansion of taxis, more private car ownership	Rapid expansion in taxis and car ownership. Introduction of second-hand trams and buses from France, Switzerland, former East Germany and Hungary	Continued rise of private car ownership, improvements to public transport – new trams, trolleybuses, etc. New metro line opened
industry	Large-scale, state-owned. Large factories located within the city	Large-scale, state-owned. Early reform (not privatisation) involved job losses and released many people into job market. Some factories closed altogether	Further closure and restructuring of state-owned industries, e.g. engineering Some small-scale industries developed	Diversification and major growth of new industries, e.g. information and communications technology hardware and software. Internet brought explosion of internet cafés to the streets (most people do not own computers)
revitalisation	Large-scale, planned development of suburbs and the city centre (*Centru Civic* plans initiated by Ceaucescu)	Little development/ re-development. *Centru Civic* plans abandoned	Local area initiatives, historical quarters, e.g. Strada Lipscani, semi-pedestrianised and cobbled. Famous old buildings such as Manuc's Inn restored	Western European influences in regeneration more widespread, e.g. construction of financial plazas, new hotels

Figure 25: Bucharest city centre.

- - - City boundary in 1938	Civic centre	Apartment blocks
—— Main boulevards	Historic centre	Lakes
—⊢—■ Railway		

Housing

After 1989 restrictions on the movement of people were lifted and many people migrated to Bucharest from smaller towns and cities in search of employment, thus the population of the city grew rapidly. This led to a massive housing shortage and the problem was exacerbated by the fact that many apartment blocks were in a very poor condition. Immediately after the Revolution it became possible for the owners of apartments to buy them cheaply from the state. A housing market quickly developed and as some areas of the city became more desirable than others, so their property prices rose. As a result, the differences between desirable and less desirable areas became more marked, and inequalities (which communism had tried to eliminate) in terms of the 'haves' and 'have nots' began to increase.

Many of the people who can afford it are moving out of apartment blocks in the city centre to houses and villas in the suburbs. This process of suburbanisation is similar to that which occurred in the UK in the 1950s – and has resulted in increasing pressure being placed upon agricultural land at the edge of the city for house building. There is also a rising demand among business people for high-quality, luxury housing. One response to this has been the construction of growth nodes and private villages ('gated communities') in the urban periphery, for example Baneasa Residential Park near the city's two airports. Baneasa Residential Park covers an area of 112,000 sq m and contains 97 villas (see www.baneasaresidentialpark.ro).

Transport

In spite of improvements in public transport within Bucharest, there has been a massive increase in car ownership. This is mainly due to the fact that levels of personal wealth have risen, but is also partly because restrictions on ownership have been lifted. One consequence of this increase is that what were already high levels of air pollution in the city have risen even further.

Industry

After 1989 substantial industrial restructuring took place and levels of unemployment rose in Bucharest where the impacts of de-industrialisation and the closure of many large-scale traditional industries were similar to those experienced in the UK during the late 1970s and early 1980s. However, new enterprises have been attracted to the city, such as computer hardware and software companies, in part because of the ready supply of cheap labour. Since 1996 the city centre has been transformed. In 2000, following a (very unpopular) decision to regulate their operations, the kiosks which had so dominated the city's streets began to disappear.

Revitalisation

Some attempts have been made to improve the appearance of the historic centre of the city. Strada Lipscani has been pedestrianised and re-paved, buildings cleaned and restored, and modern street lighting installed. The historic Hanul Lui Manuc (Manuc's Inn) has also been restored and the area around it semi pedestrianised. Although at times imitating the heritage approach to regeneration which has been common in western Europe, for example in Freiburg in Germany, Colmar in France, Dublin in the Republic of Ireland, some of Bucharest's revitalisation schemes have included contemporary design.

The range and variety of shops is growing all the time. In 1999 a new, Turkish-owned shopping mall 'The Bucharest Mall' was opened. The mall includes shops that are found in many European cities, e.g. Marks & Spencer, The Body Shop; and elsewhere in the city are outlets for other trans-national corporations such as Pizza Hut and McDonald's. These give the city a 'universal' feel (Figure 26). Modern buildings, such as the high-rise offices in the financial district, are also universal in style. However, part of the architectural legacy from the communist era includes buildings influenced by North Korean styles, thus, Bucharest contains much that is distinctive. This distinctiveness is an asset, and gives Bucharest an image which is saleable in an increasingly competitive world.

Further information on Bucharest may be found at the following websites

- http://www.pmb.ro – Interactive map of Bucharest
- www.bucharest.go.ro – Welcome to Bucharest
- www.inyourpocket.com/Romania/Bucharest_home.shtml – Bucharest in your pocket. An online guidebook
- www.turism.ro/bucuresti/htm – Ministry of Tourism, Bucharest

Bucharest is one example of a city where change has been profound and rapid, due not only to its political history, but also to its being subjected to the same processes that affect cities around the world.

Figure 26: Unirea Shopping Centre, Bucharest. Photo: Janet Speake.

Activity Box 21: Bucharest: a city in transition

Until the Second World War, Bucharest was very similar to other European cities. In 1945 the Communist party seized control. From 1945-89, development was distinctly state-planned and there was very little innovation. There was very little exposure to influences from the western world, in common with other countries behind the Iron Curtain. By western standards the basic urban fabric in 1989 was old, obsolete and outdated. Since 1989 Bucharest has been turning itself into a global capital city and trying to do in a decade what other cities have taken half a century to do. The faster pace of change has occurred because the intermediate stages of development have been unnecessary and therefore omitted. For residents the pace of change has been almost breathless. The table below illustrates and describes these changes. Consider the description and questions that relate to each image.

Images of Bucharest	Commentary and task
 Resident using mobile phone. Photo: Daniela Dumbraveanu.	In 1996 there was 0% mobile phone ownership in Bucharest. The first networks opened in 1997. In 2001 there were around 3 million mobile phone subscribers. Nationally this represents about 14% of the population. It is possible to estimate that the ownership rates in Bucharest are double this. The mobile phone is important as an ultimate status symbol as well as a means of communication. Although they are expensive for most Romanians they would go without essential goods in order to be seen to own a mobile phone. ■ For aspiring young Romanians what does the mobile phone symbolise which makes it so popular? ■ How does this compare to how you perceive the importance of mobile phones?
 Internet café. Photo: Janet Speake.	The first internet café in Bucharest opened in 1997 and by 2002 there were over 50. Significantly the internet cafés are found all over the city (including areas of housing blocks) and not just in the city centre. Only about 4% of the population in Romania use the internet and most do not have access to it at home. ■ Why do you think internet cafés are so popular? ■ Look closely at the image. How does it show that Bucharest is subject to the impacts of globalisation? ■ Why is it important for people and businesses to be able to connect with the global information highway?

Activity Box 21: Bucharest: a city in transition (continued)

Bucharest Shopping Mall. Photo: Duncan Light.

- Are you surprised that Bucharest has a western style shopping mall?
- How does this show another example of globalisation?
- Only the very rich can afford to shop at this mall, nevertheless, whatever time of the day or night it is always crowded. Can you say why this is?

Benetton and kiosks. Photo: Duncan Light.

This image shows the two forms of retailing in contemporary Bucharest. Benetton (the trans-national clothing corporation) has had branches in Bucharest since the mid-1990s. Kiosks sell everyday goods and are locally owned.

- How does this image illustrate the growing polarisation between rich and poor in the city?

High-rise buildings in Strada Doamnei. Photo: Duncan Light.

During the last five years several new high-rise buildings have been constructed in Bucharest. New high-rise buildings are being built within the old city centre with little regard for their historic setting.

- In what ways are such buildings trying to make a statement about the city?
- Why do you think that conservation is given such a low priority?

New tram. Photo: Duncan Light.

In all cities image is crucial in attracting investment and tourists. In the last few years, the dilapidated trams inherited from the socialist period have largely been replaced.

- Why would these old trams have been bad for the image of the city?
- What do you think the appearance of the new trams does for the city's image?

CHAPTER 7

CONTINUING DYNAMICS

City centres are in a constant state of change. Economic, political and social forces operating at international, national and local scales continue to determine their development. With 'globalisation' has come increasing uniformity in the types of products people buy, the places they buy them in, and the ways in which they spend their leisure time. The result is an increasing uniformity in many aspects of city centre geographies. Cities are in competition with one another for inward investment and so strive to enhance their image on all fronts, identifying their 'positive' and 'attractive' features and characteristics (particularly those which distinguish them from other cities). Of these features, cultural ones (e.g. a new art gallery, theatre or 'cultural quarter') are increasingly important in the post-industrial and post-modern city.

The dynamic nature of urban change has been likened to objects as diverse as kaleidoscopes or tornadoes. In a kaleidoscope, the distribution of colours and shapes is ever changing, but has some regularity, as is the form and function of cities. Tornadoes, like cities, develop rapidly and travel in a broadly, but not wholly, predictable direction. They move objects around in a random way and often deposit them in unexpected places. This analogy helps to explain why it is that most models of urban form produced in the early part of the twentieth century are no longer appropriate for the study of contemporary western cities. New and different approaches are needed, such as those of Hall (1998), Short (1996) and Ellin (1999), all of whom have explored the ideas associated with post-modern urbanism and the way these relate to the nature of contemporary cities in many part of the world. The post-modern city, for example, is one in which change is constant and often unpredictable, driven less by large-scale planning decisions and more by smaller-scale entrepreneurialism.

What is viewed as 'progress' in city centre development may have negative as well as positive impacts. For example, the gentrification process may enhance the appearance of previously run-down areas, but also displace or destroy traditional social and economic structures. These types of change can trigger a reduction in, or disappearance of, what is known as the 'organic' driver for change, that is the effect in which part of a city generates its own impetus for development and change. An example of this is the Hoxton Square area of Shoreditch, London. Artists were attracted to live in Hoxton Square, partly because of the relatively low price of property there, and because it became the centre of a cluster of successful 'Young British Artists' in the 1990s. However, many artists have since moved out of the area as it became colonised by café-bars, restaurants and 'yuppies', and property prices soared (*The Observer*, 2001).

Social exclusion is one consequence of rapid urban transition of the kind described in this book, as urban society becomes more polarised with the very affluent at one end of the spectrum and the poor at the other. Areas associated with each of these extremes may sometimes be juxtaposed, as is the case of Woolton (affluent) and Netherley (less affluent) in Liverpool. Similarly, in Manchester at the same time that a city-centre apartment was sold for £1 million early in 2001, only 3km away some terraced houses were on the market for £4000. The increasing polarisation of rich and poor is an issue which most cities face and will have to deal with in order to improve the quality of life for all residents. There are cases in some cities in the west where a failure to address the issue of social exclusion and polarisation has resulted in the creation of a disillusioned and often angry 'underclass' of people who feel that they have no place in, or meaningful input into, contemporary society.

Current approaches to the development and regeneration of cities and their centres frequently involve consultation with local people and organisations, as well as other interested parties, whose ideas and decisions are fed into the planning process. Most cities have instigated economic development initiatives some of which are 'top-down' (e.g. decisions taken by city councils and large organisations), others 'bottom-up' (e.g. activities which include community decision making), and yet others a mixture of the two. It is now also common for regeneration programmes to involve consultations with young people like yourself, many of whom are active members of young 'urbanist' groups that have a vital input into discussions relating to the future of your cities. As well as having a finger on the pulse of contemporary fashions and trends, you are the inheritors of today's decisions, so your input is crucial to the decision-making process.

The form and functions of city-centres have undergone considerable change in the last few decades, and the rate and unpredictability of change is increasing, thus making it difficult to plan ahead.

For example, back in the 1980s few could have predicted the impact of the information and communications revolution on the form, function and ways of life in city centres around the world. The same unpredictability faces us now – apart from knowing that our cities will be influenced by processes and decisions taken at international as well as national and local levels, we can only guess at their precise nature, and of the final outcome. This is not to say that planning is a pointless exercise; rather that urban designers need to take account of the need for flexibility both in the way that city spaces are used, and in the way they are designed.

REFERENCES AND FURTHER READING

References

Blackpool Borough Council (1999) *Agenda 2000: A case for structural fund eligibility.* Blackpool: Blackpool BC.

Burford, T. and Richardson, D. (1998) *Romania: The rough guide.* London: Penguin.

City of Manchester Planning Department (1986) *Changes in Manufacturing in the City of Manchester (A sectoral survey)* Economic Briefing Note 73. Manchester: Manchester City Council.

Davis, M. (1990) *City of Quartz: Excavating the future in Los Angeles.* London: Verso.

Ellin, N. (1999) *Postmodern Urbanism.* Princeton: Princeton Architectural Press.

Fawcett, A. (2001) 'Blackpool gambles on becoming a Lancashire Las Vegas', *Business North West*, February.

Hall, T. (1998) *Urban Geography.* London: Routledge.

Holden, A. (2001) 'Welcome to Vegas-on-Sea', *The Times*, 19 July.

Kivell, P. (1993) *Land Use and the City: Patterns and processes of urban change.* London: Routledge.

Light, D. and Speake, J. (2000) 'Heritage tourism and urban regeneration: a sustainable solution?' in Ianos, I., Pumain, D. and Racine, J.B. (eds) *Integrated Urban Systems and Sustainability of Urban Life.* Bucharest: Editura Tehnica, pp. 101-11.

Malbon, B. (1998) 'The club. Clubbing, consumption, identity and the spatial practices of every-night life' in Skelton, T. and Valentine, G. (eds) *Cool Places: Geographies of youth cultures.* London: Routledge, pp. 266-86.

Oc, T. and Tiesdell (1997) *Safer City Centres.* London: Chapman.

Short, J.R. (1996) *The Urban Order: An introduction to cities, culture and power.* Oxford: Blackwell.

Soja, E. (1995) 'Postmodern urbanization: the six restructurings of Los Angeles' in Watson, S. and Gibbs, K. (eds) *Postmodern Cities and Spaces.* Oxford: Blackwell, pp. 385-7.

Speake, J. and Donert, K. (1998) 'Approaches to investigating the geography of crime', *Teaching Geography*, 22, 1, pp. 5-9

Taylor, M. (2000) 'Last throw of the dice', *Insider North West*, 10, 9 September.

The Observer (2001) 'Young, gifted and priced out of the area they made famous', 9 September.

Tiesdell, S., Oc, T. and Heath, T. (1996) *Revitalizing Historic Urban Quarters.* Oxford: Architectural Press.

Walford, R. (1997) *Land Use UK: A survey for the 21st century.* Sheffield: Geographical Association.

Wynne-Jones, R. (1997) 'One motorway, two Britains' *The Independent on Sunday*, 11 May.

Zukin, S. (1996) *The Cultures of Cities.* Oxford: Blackwell.

Further reading

Allen, J., Massey, D. and Pryke, M. (1999) *Unsettling Cities.* London: Routledge.

Carpenter, J. and Lees, L. (1995) 'Gentrification in New York, London and Paris: an international comparison', *International Journal of Urban and Regional Research*, 19, pp. 286-306.

Gordon, D.L.A. (1996) 'Planning design and managing change in urban waterfront redevelopment', *Town Planning Review*, 67, pp. 261-90.

Hall, T. and Hubbard, P. (1996) *The Art of Regeneration: Urban renewal through cultural activities* (A Comedia report). Stroud: Comedia.

Kearns, G. and Philo, C. (eds) (1993) *Selling Places: The city as cultural capital, past and present.* Oxford: Pergamon.

King, A. (ed) (1996) *Re-Presenting the City.* London: McMillan.

Massey, D., Allen, J. and Pile, S. (1998) *City Worlds.* London: Routledge.

Miles, M. (1997) *Art, Space and the City: Public art and urban futures.* London: Routledge.

Pacione, M. (1997) *Britain's Cities: Geographies of division in urban Britain.* London: Routledge.

Pacione, M. (2001a) 'Models of land use structure in cities of the developed world', *Geography*, 86, 2, pp. 97-120.

Pacione, M. (2001b) 'The internal structure of cities in the third world', *Geography*, 86, 3, pp. 189-210.

Pacione, M. (2001c) 'The future of the city – cities of the future', *Geography*, 86, 4, pp. 275-86.

Pacione, M. (2001d) *Urban Geography.* London: Routledge.

Pile, S., Brook, C. and Mooney, G. (eds) (1999) *Unruly Cities.* London: Routledge.

Roberts, P. and Sykes, H. (eds) (2000) *Urban Regeneration: A handbook.* London: Sage.

Rogers, R. and Power, A. (2000) *Cities for a Small Country.* Cambridge: Cambridge University Press.

Smyth, H. (1994) *Marketing the City: The role of flagship developments in urban regeneration.* London: Spon.

Speake, J. and Fox, V. (2000) 'Investigating culturally-led regeneration', *Teaching Geography*, 25, 2, pp. 56-60.

Turnock, D. (1990) 'Bucharest', *Cities*, May, pp. 107-18.

Urry, J. (1995) *Consuming Places.* London: Routledge.

Valentine, G. (2001) *Social Geographies: Space and society.* London: Prentice Hall.

Zukin, S. (1991) *Landscapes of Power: From Detroit to Disney World.* Berkeley and Los Angeles: University of California Press.

Websites

- http://www.pmb.ro – Interactive map of Bucharest
- www.baneasearesidentialpark.ro – Baneasea Residential Park, Bucharest.
- www.berlin.de/ – Guide to Berlin.
- www.blackpool.gov.uk – Local government information on Blackpool.
- www.blackpooltourism.com – Publicity material on Blackpool.
- www.bucharest.go.ro – Welcome to Bucharest.
- www.ctiweb.cf.ac.uk – CTI Centre for the Built Environment.
- www.greatbuildings.com – Pictorial presentation of a selection of the world's greatest buildings.
- www.inyourpocket.com/Romania/Bucharest_home.shtml – Bucharest in your pocket – online guidebook.
- www.regenerationmagazine.com – Regeneration and Renewal (weekly electronic magazine).
- www.rudi.herts.ac.uk – Resource for Urban Design Information.
- www.turism.ro/bucuresti/htm – Ministry of Tourism, Bucharest.